Killing Cats Leads To Rats

Published by Motivational Press, Inc.
1777 Aurora Road
Melbourne, Florida, 32935
www.MotivationalPress.com

ISBN: 978-1-62865-520-9

Killing Cats
Leads to Rats

Richard Franzi

MOtivational PRESS®
LEADERS IN GLOBAL PUBLISHING

—— Table of Contents ——

I dedicate this book to my mother and father, who made many sacrifices to ensure that my brother and I had a solid foundation from which to live the American Dream.

Foreword
by Marshall Goldsmith

Killing Cats Leads to Rats by Richard Franzi is an incredibly poignant foray into the realm of unintended consequences caused by intentional actions taken by organizations. Well written, factual, and insightful, I thoroughly enjoyed learning from Richard!

For instance, Richard describes the "Law of Unintended Consequences". This is not something that most leaders think too much about. Most are so focused on the outcome of their decisions that they may neglect what could happen as a result of the actions they direct others to take.

Just getting started in the first part of this important work of leadership literature, Richard describes Dr. Robert K. Merton's description of three types of unanticipated consequences. First are "negative effects which are contrary to the original intentions". Second are "catalysts for future problems, or the snowball effect also known as 'Murphy's Law.'" Third are "positive benefits, which are unexpected and are often referred to as 'serendipity' or 'luck.'" When leaders make decisions with all three of these types of consequences in mind, their decisions are better, stronger, less prone to result in negative and unplanned outcomes.

Diving even deeper into unintended consequences, Richard

explores the five causes of them. I'll leave it to you to read the descriptions of these and how they apply, but I will give you the list here as I find it absolutely imperative to know them and fascinating to learn about them. The five causes of unintended consequences according to Richard are: ignorance, error, immediate interests, basic values, and self-fulfilling prophecy.

Enjoy learning about these causes of unexpected and unintended consequences and so much more as you read Richard Franzi's incredibly helpful book, *Killing Cats Leads to Rats!*

Life is good.

Marshall Goldsmith

International best-selling author or editor of 36 books including *What Got You Here Won't Get You There* and *Triggers*

Section I:
Why Killing Cats Leads to Rats

1
Unintended Consequences Can Be A Beastly Problem

"There are downsides to everything; there are unintended consequences to everything."

—Steve Jobs

IN THE SPRING OF 1992, TENS OF THOUSANDS OF enraged citizens took to the streets in the Philippines, some of them armed with grenades, Molotov cocktails, and bombs. Three people were killed by a blast in Davao City; 40 trucks were burned to wreckage. The streets of Manila seethed with fire, the flames mirroring the frustration and contempt in the people's eyes.

Who could have guessed that bottle caps could ignite such anger?

To be fair, it wasn't the caps' fault. The riots, rage, and deaths were the tragic results of a marketing campaign gone wrong: Pepsi-Cola Philippine Inc.'s "ingenious plan" that would be remembered as *The Number Fever*. It had begun as an opportunistic yet well-intentioned ploy after marketing experts shrewdly pinpointed two local money-making factors: the native citizens' cultural inclination for gambling and the universal attraction to get-rich-quick promises.

Playing up on those elements, the company strategically numbered the underside of some of their best-selling products—Pepsi, Mountain

Dew, and 7-Up—with the promise of a cash prize ranging from 1,000–1,000,000 pesos. The one million pesos, of course, would be given to *one* very lucky winner who would be announced at the promotion's end.

As the campaign went viral, it had all the trappings to become a massive success. And initially, it was.

In the 1990s, Coca-Cola had been outselling Pepsi-Cola; the former had 75% of the market share, while the latter was grappling to scale up to 17%. Within two weeks of the "lucky number" campaign, Pepsi-Cola's sales catapulted up to 40%. Likely jumping up and down with joy in their offices, the top executives of Pepsi-Cola decided to stretch their luck. Seeking to extend the reach of the campaign across the nation, they increased the quantity of prizes, promising that there would be up to 1,500 winners. By the promotion's end, it was estimated that they'd amassed 31 million participants—over half of the country's population at the time.

All good things must come to an end, of course. Pepsi-Cola's competition terminated two months later. It was time to announce a winner.

Soon after Pepsi-Cola finally announced that the million-pesos-winning number was "349", its executives realized that they had made a horrendous mistake. In their original strategy, they'd agreed to *not* consider certain numbers for the competition, "349" being among them. The consultants somehow missed the memo. They'd printed 800,000 bottle caps with that exact number.

Hundreds of thousands of locals immediately flocked to Pepsi-Cola's offices, righteously demanding their one million pesos. In an effort to cover up their blunder, Pepsi-Cola initially tried to convince the customers that their caps were invalid, saying that they lacked the correct security code. Then the company tried to blame the mistake on a technical glitch, explaining that their computer program had selected the number by mistake. It didn't help matters that a similar "number fever" had erupted throughout Chile only one month prior after a faulty fax released the wrong winning number and ended in public (but nonlethal) outcry.

That's when all hell broke loose in the Philippines.[i]

The Universality of Unintended Consequences

My personal fascination with the concept of unintended consequences in the business world manifested in 2009. While hosting the Critical Mass Radio Show and speaking to a variety of entrepreneurs and CEOs, I was privy to a spectrum of intriguing anecdotes by my guests. These men and women shared with me how the actual outcomes of many of their strategic initiatives contrasted sharply with their predicted outcomes. They confided in me the unintended outcomes that emerged as detrimental consequences: everything from ruined employee morale to undermined company performance.

Within me sprouted a nagging question: *Why?* And then: *Can't we avoid this?*

To a degree, *yes*, we can. But to avoid a problem, we must first acknowledge it for what it is. We must recognize it in its true form and define it.

These interviews propelled me to begin my own journey of discovery. I wanted to dig to the root of the cause, and I also wanted to find a way to help business executives anticipate and predict more carefully the outcomes of their decisions. I realized that the stage of anticipating and predicting was just as essential to success as was the second stage of implementing and achieving. If you don't know where you're going, how the heck will you know when you've gotten there? And even when you *do* have a pin dropped on your GPS map, you better check out Google Earth before you gear up for your roadtrip just to make sure you aren't headed for a swamp full of quicksand.

---

i   https://i1.wp.com/arpitsrivastava.files.wordpress.com/2013/07/pepsi-fiasco-3.jpg?resize=485%2C353

"If I had only one hour to save the world, I would spend ffty-fve minutes defning the problem, and only fve minutes fnding the solution."
—Albert Einstein

Unintended consequences are, more often than not, the result of misunderstandings and miscalculations. They emerge due to human error, often due to the fallacy that we've thoroughly thought things through when we actually haven't.

Case in point? Here's a grim one (literally).

In Europe, the Grim Reaper had his hands especially full in the years 1346–1353—the peak of the Black Plague pandemic, which has been heralded as one of the most devastating pandemics in human history. It's estimated that 75 million people—a staggering 30% of Europe's population at the time—died from the Plague. It is generally agreed that the pandemic originated in Asia and was transferred to Europe via the Silk Road trade route. Whatever the entry point, most experts have since agreed that the Plague was caused by fleas on the rats that infested the region's merchant ships. Many historians also agree that there were several contributing factors to the scale of the pandemic, including the killing of one certain animal.

Cats.

I suppose you could say the craze partially began with Pope Gregory IX, originally a skilled lawyer who reigned as the Pope from 1227–1241; in the 1230s, he issued the papal edict *vox in rama*, which is the reason why black cats are stereotyped to this day as carriers of bad luck (or, in that pope's terms, "vessels for Satan's spirit"). By condemning black cats, Pope Gregory IX practically signed their death warrant. His bias, like all forms of unchecked bias, spread to infect the rest of society, ultimately resulting in a widespread fear of cats as associates of witches, causing the persecution of both humans and animals in the years leading up to the Black Plague and later the Great Plague of London.

Fast-forward to the Great Plague of London. By then, people were freely exterminating both cats and dogs, fearing that these animals were the carriers of the pandemic. On July 1, 1665, the Lord Mayor of London, Sir William Lawrence, published the Lord Mayor Orders—a decree backed by the encouragement of multiple physicians (with most if not all of them likely having the best intentions for mankind)—that all dogs and cats had to be immediately slaughtered in hopes of eliminating the Plague. Men were employed to become dog- and cat-killers; they ended the lives of tens of thousands of cats and dogs.

This did not stop the Plague as was the intention. On the contrary, it fueled it.

Killing cats leads to rats. That's the moral of the story here. Cats and dogs were the natural predators of rats; without them, the disease-ridden flea-infested rats were free to flourish. Recordings show that 267 Londoners died in the last week of June, the week before the issue of the Lord Mayor Orders. Exactly one month later, 1,843 Londoners died during the last week of July.

Through a foolish decree, the human death rate hadn't doubled or even tripled. It'd been multiplied by *six*.

"An ounce of prevention is worth a pound of cure."
—Benjamin Franklin

These are not business examples, obviously, but are exemplary of human fallacy and miscalculation; I've come to realize over the years that the concept of unintended consequences applies *everywhere*. The faulty strategies to contain the Black Plague and the Great Plague of London are simply two vivid examples of the power and extent that unintended consequences can have, and especially how easily they can inflate to a monumental scale. Like rodents, unintended consequences don't discriminate between the size of a place or the number of employees involved; they can just as easily overtake and overturn a small family business as they can a conglomerate empire. Like rodents, they can chew through the fabric of your company, damaging the business's reputation, diminishing the company's performance, undermining the employees' confidence in executive leadership, and causing clients to avoid your company like the Plague.

Remember the fiasco of "the Number Fever" of 1992, described at the beginning of this chapter? Realizing that they had been duped— and not caring how accidently it had been done—the Filipino people's wrath manifested itself in fires, bombs, grenades, and violence; at least three people died and six were severely wounded. Pepsi-Cola's company property was destroyed, with dozens of their delivery trucks torched or stoned—and, worse, their brand tarnished and their reputation tattered. Over 22,000 people filed lawsuits against Pepsi-Cola, also filing over 5,200 criminal complaints on the grounds of fraud and deception. By the end of this madness, Pepsi-Cola's budget of $2 million for prize payouts morphed into a staggering $10 million price-tag in restitution and legal fees. It took *fourteen years* for the Supreme Court of the Philippines to clear Pepsi-Cola of all criminal charges.

Talk about unintended consequences.

Throughout this book, I'll be sharing with you a wide spectrum of business anecdotes to help illustrate the frequency and variety of unintended consequences in the business world. Such consequences are a massive challenge that all business leaders must face and overcome… each individual time. In retrospect, some of these stories might seem humorous—even ridiculous. Others may perplex you, as you wonder how nobody saw them coming. Hindsight vision, they say, is always 20/20. It'll make you wonder, too—especially after reading about giants ranging from Starbucks to Pfizer to General Motors to Samsung—if anyone is actually immune.

There's no silver bullet or foolproof protection that executives can use to permanently prevent unintended consequences from infesting their business decisions. While no one actually wields a truly functioning crystal ball (if I'm wrong, you're welcome to introduce me to such a person!) and it is impossible for us to always accurately calculate the consequences of our actions, we *can* arm ourselves with the information, safeguard measures, and judgment needed to better predict and ideally control the outcomes of our strategic decisions. Being proactive is half the battle.

And so, within the following chapters, I'd like to share with you my discovery of the key environmental conditions which breed negative unintended impacts. By defining the danger zones, you'll be better able to equip yourself with the mentality and methods needed to prevent and control them. By implementing specific and powerful best practices, you can effectively minimize and even eradicate such effects on your business performance.

That said, it's time to introduce you to Dr. Robert K. Merton.

2
Meet Dr. Merton

"The most obvious limitation to a correct anticipation of consequences of action is provided by the existing state of knowledge."

—Robert K. Merton

EMERGING FROM THE U.S.'S GREAT RECESSION, INItiated by the housing market's bubble-bursting and the subprime mortgage crisis in mid-2007 to 2009, America's brick-and-mortar stores suddenly found themselves losing ground to online retailers. To retaliate, many of them focused on Black Friday, the kickoff to the holiday sales season known to account for up to 40% of some retailers' sales. It could be, they reasoned, the logical stepping stone that would help them rise and reign again as top players in the industry.

That's why, in 2011, Target decided to open at midnight to kick off its Black Friday sales. One year later, like several other of its competitors, the company opened its doors a few hours earlier, on the evening of Thanksgiving Day. From a business perspective, it seemed like a straightforward fork in the road: either keep up in a competitive, cutthroat market or lose ground. Choosing to prioritize the company's revenue, Target executives believed that opening their stores on Thanksgiving afternoon would be best for the business.

The initial statistics agreed with this sentiment, showing an increase in overall traffic and sales. Except...the decision came packaged with a heavy unintended consequence. Target employees complained that the early opening hours ruined their holidays, a poignant argument especially powerful because it regarded the family-oriented holiday of Thanksgiving. In today's age of rampant social media, the employees publicized their complaints easily and immediately, resulting in a Change.org petition titled "Target: Take the High Road and Save Thanksgiving". This petition amassed over 300,000 signatures.

A bullseye success? Hardly. For the first time since its establishment, Target had faltered gravely from its mark.

Robert K. Merton: A Founding Father of Modern Sociology

American sociologist, writer, and Columbia University professor Robert K. Merton (1910–2003) coined the terms "unintended consequences", "role model", "reference group", and "self-fulfilling prophecy" among others. Having developed a number of central elements in sociological, political, and economic theory, Merton is considered a founding father of modern sociology. He pioneered with studies in the fields of deviance, communications, social psychology, social stratification, social structure, and bureaucracy; in 1994, he won the National Medal of Science for his contributions. His work proved pivotal for defining the discipline and for the emergence of several sociology subfields in the mid-20th century.

As a "functional sociologist", Merton viewed society as an organism composed of various parts, with each part responsible for specific functions: some intentional, others unintentional, and several disruptive. The functionalist perspective, as detailed in John Macionis and Ken Plummer's *Sociology: A Global Introduction* envisages society as a complex system whose parts collaborate to promote solidarity and stability, with our individual lives guided by "relatively stable patterns of social behavior" (social structure).[ii] When all parts are in sync, society runs smoothly; if one cog in the cogwheel sticks, it disrupts the entire gear.[iii]

Merton's perspective on a properly functioning society can easily correlate to the smaller ecosystem of a work environment—for instance, when paralleling the bureaucratic structure in society with that of modern privately held businesses and corporations. In his book *Social Theory and Social Structure,* Merton explains how most bureaucratic offices "involve the expectation of life-long tenure, in the absence of disturbing factors which may decrease the size of the organization" and, if they are to function successfully, must attain a "high degree of reliability of behavior, and unusual degree of conformity with prescribed patterns of action [...] buttressed by strong sentiments which entail devotion to one's duties, a keen sense of the limitation of one's authority and competence, and methodical performance of routine activities."[iv]

He defines the central orientation of functionalism through the practice of interpreting data by establishing their consequences for larger structures in which they are implicated, classifying this into two types of functions:

- **Manifest functions:** objective consequences contributing to the adjustment or adaptation of the system as intended and recognized by the system participants.

---

ii   Macionis, J. J., % Plummer, K. (2012). *Sociology: A global introduction* (5th ed.). Harlow: Pearson Prentice Hall.

iii   Sobal, L. (2016, September 15). The Dilemma of Unintended Consequences of Public Policy on Health Care. Retrieved from https://www.medaxiom.com/blog/the-dilemma-of-unintended-consequences-of-public-policy-on-health-care.

iv   Merton, R. K. (1968). *Social theory and social structure.* New York: Free Press.

- **Latent functions:** consequences which are neither intended nor recognized, which also contribute to the system's adjustment.[v]

Through this framework of functional sociology, Merton delved into the concept of unanticipated consequences of social action, eventually making this the underlying theme of his work. In his 1936 essay "The Unanticipated Consequences of Purposive Social Action," Merton describes that we are typically aware of our intentions (intended consequences) and can explain them; on the other hand, unintended consequences are not as easy to define or recognize. Ignorance and error, Merton argues, are the primary factors of the latter, accounting for social movements developing in utterly unanticipated directions. He argues that this can and should be countered by a systematic and objective analysis of the development of unanticipated consequences of purposive social action, "the treatment of which has for much too long been consigned to the realm of theology and speculative philosophy."[vi]

Merton's brainchild, the Law of Unintended Consequences, was thus born.

"Unintended consequences get to the heart of why you never really understand an adaptive problem until you have solved it. Problems morph and 'solutions' often point to deeper problems. In social life, as in nature, we are walking on a trampoline. Every inroad reconfgures the environment we tread on."

—Robert Pascale

---

v   Elwell, F. (n.d.). Robert K. Merton in His Own Words. Retrieved from http://www.faculty.rsu.edu/users/f/felwell/www/presentations/MertonWords.html.

vi   Merton, R. K. (1936, December). The Unanticipated Consequences of Purposive Social Action. *American Sociological Review, 1*(6), 894-904.

The Three Types of Unintended Consequences

The Law of Unintended Consequences transcends time and place. Akin to Murphy's Law, the Law of Unintended Consequences has become an idiomatic warning that intervening in a complex system tends to ensue in unanticipated and unwanted outcomes; it argues against the belief that we humans fully control the world around us. I will interpret the law to mean that, for businesses, human purposeful actions have *at least one* unanticipated or unintended consequence, and that every cause (i.e. strategic decision) has *more than one* possible outcome, including those that are unforeseen outcomes.

In his research, Merton differentiated unanticipated consequences and classified them as three types:

1. **Negative effects**, which are contrary to the original intentions. One popular example is the Cobra Effect: back when India was a British colony, the government initiated a program that rewarded people for killing venomous cobra snakes in Delhi. For a while, lots of snakes were indeed killed and their hunters were rewarded. Then cobra breeders started popping up, cultivating snake farms and then killing the animals to reap rewards. The government ended the program once it realized the scheme. This resulted in the cobra breeders setting the snakes free, since those people were no longer making money off of that enterprise, immediately inflating the venomous cobra population and completely backfiring on the government's initial intentions.

2. **Catalysts for future problems**, or the snowball effect also known as "Murphy's Law". The 18th amendment to the U.S. Constitution—i.e. "Prohibition", the social reform policy intended to curb alcohol consumption and "moralize" society in the United States—may serve as an example of such a problematic decision. In the timespan between the

amendment's implementation and its repeal, New York's bars-turned-speakeasies had gone from 800 to 4,000 in number, with gangsters and criminals viewing the ban as a fantastic business opportunity. They profited immensely from the consequent bootlegging, with newspapers alleging at the time that even 80% of congressmen drank in secret.[vii] Rather than creating a "moral society", the amendment created the foundation for a new era of bootleggers and criminals amidst a society that was now more likely to drink in secret, commend its gangsters, support its criminals, and embrace immorality.

3. **Positive benefits**, which are still unexpected and are often referred to as "serendipity" or "luck." One of the most famous instances of serendipity is the discovery of penicillin through accidental contamination of laboratory samples. An example in the business world began when 29-year-old Howard Schultz was sent by his boss to Milan on a business trip and was thus exposed to that Italian city's lively espresso bars. Schultz trashed his boss's to-do list and instead returned with the idea to create an espresso bar chain in America. His boss disapproved, so Schultz decided to pursue the idea himself; the global phenomenon of Starbucks emerged from that one random business trip. "Good luck in business is hard work" is a wise adage, because a seed of luck will never flourish if you don't recognize and cultivate it. Serendipity is the luck we attract to ourselves, some experts say; Thomas Jefferson himself is quoted to have said: "I'm a great believer in luck, and I find the harder I work, the more I have of it."

---

vii   Sandbrook, D. (2012, August 25). How Prohibition backfired and gave America an era of gangsters and speakeasies. Retrieved from https://www.theguardian.com/film/2012/aug/26/lawless-prohibition-gangsters-speakeasies.

The Decision Ecosystem

I've partially based my exploration of unintended consequences in business on Dr. Merton's lifelong research regarding unanticipated consequences in social systems. I've found commonalities and translated them to the business system, which is similarly a collection of people who undertake (in Merton's terms) **purposeful action** to achieve desired outcomes. I did realize, however, that something was missing: a critical element in the business process leading up to the initiation of purposeful action by a company's employees.

I've coined this "**the decision ecosystem**" (Decision EcoSystem™).

The decision ecosystem is basically the environment—including people and resources—surrounding an executive, which influences and aids him or her in formulating his or her framework for any strategic decision that will lead to purposeful action. I've noted that improvements in the robustness of the decision ecosystem lead to a respective reduction in the probability of unintended consequences ensuing from the executive's decision.

Makes sense, right? The more robust the ecosystem, the better. That's because your decision is only as good as the information which you base it upon.

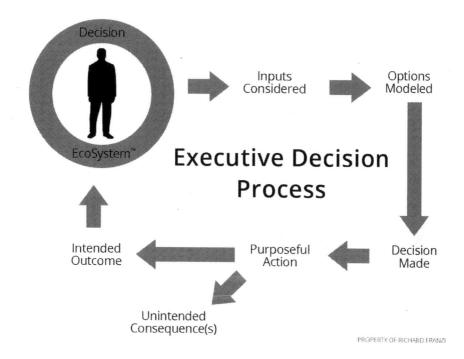

All executives have a decision ecosystem, whether they are aware of it or not. To make optimal decisions, it is essential for them to carefully analyze how healthy that environment is and how capable it is to provide the support and information required for the necessary decisions. One of the most telling characteristics of a powerful and sound decision ecosystem is the existence of a transparent and intelligent infusion of peer executive input and advice. It's certainly not the only key element, however; when faced with major decisions, executives must consider a variety of inputs in order to model a variety of scenarios that their decision could create, thereby proactively examining them and choosing the most desirable path. When this happens, the decision leads to the correct purposeful action (especially on the part of the employees) specifically designed to achieve the expected outcome.

Which, while expected, isn't necessarily achieved.

As smooth of a process as it sounds, this is fertile ground in which unintended consequences can fester and develop. Understanding how and why these accidental outcomes occur is the only thing that will enable us to control them, to reduce and as much as possible eliminate the probability of them occurring, or at the very least to minimize their negative impacts on the business.

Deciding upon and implementing an optimal strategic business decision is inherently complex, especially when many variables must be taken into account. As aforementioned, a business's operation is based on collective purposeful actions—taken by employees, suppliers, clients, and the executives themselves—to achieve the desired, predicted outcomes of the executive decision. An undeniable complexity springs from the very human nature of the people involved; each person will have his or her own understanding and interpretation of what is to be accomplished—and how.

Given this variation and the potential for misunderstandings, it's clear to see how easily your strategic decisions can be undermined by the Law of Unintended Consequences. It's also apparent to see that, due to our human nature, unintended consequences are seemingly inevitable. This is by no means an argument against our humanness, mind you, which is the bedrock for other remarkable and inherent traits that range from integrity and compassion to creativity and rational thinking. It is instead a struggle to perceive and curb the negative consequences of human fallacies. As a senior executive, you must realize that all unintended consequences can have a negative impact on your business, your reputation, and your employees' level of engagement and trust.

They are a big deal.

That much is made obvious in corporate situations such as the turmoil faced by Target in 2012. The company countered employee complaints and objections by indicating that there was no corporate policy in place which mandated that employees would work on Thanksgiving or Black Friday. They added, too, that employees who did work on that day received time-and-a-half pay. The "anti-Black Thursday movement" continued, however, as people pointed out that Thanksgiving and Black Friday were included as "blackout dates" (days when employees could not request off work).

Their arguments resonated with a public who agreed that "greed" must never trump family time. In a poll publicized by the *Chicago Tribune* a couple of years later, only 12% of Americans approved that stores revved up their big post-Thanksgiving sales by opening up on Turkey Day, with 26% disapproving of the practice and another 36% outright hating it.[viii] Target's decision ultimately hurt company morale and therefore led to bad publicity, enabling their competitors to appear more humane and likeable by making the "right choice" and giving their employees the day off.

The mess of all this fuss and retaliation is something that Target's executives may have never considered—or, even if they had, they had certainly never understood the impact and extent of such a consequence. Had they comprehended it, I believe Target's executives may have made a different decision or, or the very least, they may have considered how to gain the employees' support and involvement with the roll-out.

viii   Rosenthal, P. (2014, October 29). Christmas creep a trick and treat to boost Santa sales. *The Chicago Tribune*. Retrieved from http://www.chicagotribune.com/business/columnists/ct-christmas-creep-black-friday-sales-rosenthal-10-20141028-column.html.

3
Beware: The Five Causes of Unintended Consequences

"I want to apologize for violating the trust our customers have invested in Wells Fargo. And I want to apologize for not doing more sooner to address the causes of this unacceptable activity."
—John Stumpf, CEO of Wells Fargo

IT ALL BEGAN WITH WHAT WAS PROBABLY A well-meaning mantra. John Stumpf, the CEO of Wells Fargo, was famous for drilling his employees with the saying "eight is great", referring to his demands that his sales employees reach the target of selling at least eight products to each customer. Why eight? Well, *eight* does indeed rhyme with *great*—and that's memorable. But even though this ridiculously demanding sales culture was already near-impossible, Stumpf wanted more; in an annual report, he wrote up: "perhaps our new cheer should be *let's go again, for ten!*"

The rhyming game was strong with this one.

Up to that point, Wells Fargo & Company—a provider of personal, small business, and commercial banking based in San Francisco, California—had been doing nicely for itself in the 160+ years since its founding. Heralded as the world's second largest bank by market capitalization and the third largest bank in the U.S. by assets, Wells Fargo was named the world's most valuable bank brand in *The Banker*'s 2014 "Top 500 Banking Brands" valuation.[ix] Within the banking industry, Wells Fargo had also made a name for itself as "the King of Cross-sell", a title that paid tribute to the company's intense cross-selling strategy.

Turns out, this strategy was so intense that Wells Fargo employees were commonly berated or even fired if they failed to meet the crazy sales quota standards. According to *The Wall Street Journal*, executives would go so far as to urge employees to "hunt" for sales prospects even at bus stops and retirement homes. The executives arguably had the business's best interests at heart. After all, who wouldn't want their company to prosper? But their demands had an unforeseen consequence as these executives pushed their employees to the limit. Facing the prospect of losing their jobs, those employees started to take drastic measures.

It was eventually discovered that Wells Fargo's employees had opened an estimated 1.5–2 million bank and credit card accounts on behalf of clients *without the authorization of those clients*; this escalated to become a full-blown scandal in September of 2016. The company was charged with fraud and criminal identity theft, with the shocking scope of the scandal costing Wells Fargo over $190 million in fines and refunds, resulting in over 5,300 employee firings, and unintentionally causing tremendous injury to the company's brand and reputation.

Such stories are brilliant illustrations of the snowball effect of unintended consequences, but they can also help us extract the **five causes of unintended consequences**, as introduced by Dr. Robert K. Merton.

---

ix   Wallace, P. (2014, February 03). The Top 500 Banking Brands, 2014. *The Banker.* Retrieved from http://www.thebanker.com/Banker-Data/Banker-Rankings/The-Top-500-Banking-Brands-2014?ct=true.

- Ignorance
- Error
- Immediate Interests
- Basic Values
- Self-fulfilling Prophecy

Ignorance

Ignorance is *not* the equivalent of bliss in the business world. If you're lucky enough, you'll learn quickly from your mistakes, as did the executive team of Johnny Walker—none other than the iconic global top-seller of whiskey and the #3 premium brand worldwide by volume. This brand's intense revenue correlates to the high pricing of its versatile and vibrant whiskey portfolio, with an estimated worth of $2.5 billion in retail. Despite all its fame and prosperity, not even this goliath was insulated from the Law of Unintended Consequences.

The Johnny Walker Black label had risen to reign as the #1-selling scotch whiskey in Japan. The marketing executives, enamored by their success and craving more, decided to increase the volume of the sales and the ensuing revenue by lowering the price. In any other environment, this may have been a reasonable move. They failed, however, to take into account the cultural context of their market.

As a result, the sales of the Johnny Walker Black label plummeted. Interestingly enough, this was purely the result of the Japanese market's mentality. In Japan, the "Top 10" list of any sort of product or service is sorted primarily by price. Johnny Walker used to be the most expensive scotch whiskey in the region; due to the lowered price, it dropped to a lower ranking on Japan's list, earning the disapproval of clients who were looking for a status symbol. The brand's executives had not done their research; they were ignorant of the fact that Japanese clients strictly held the most expensive drinks in the highest esteem; when they bought someone the #1 item on such a list, it promoted the buyer's status as well as the brand's. It was as if they were telling their friend or host: "Look how important I believe you are! I think you are worthy of none other than the most expensive and therefore best scotch whiskey!"

To their credit, the Johnny Walker executives quickly caught on, reacting and raising the price. The label reverted to the top of the list; over time, so did their sales. Thanks to their quick lesson and already globally established and highly esteemed brand, Johnny Walker just got back on its feet and kept walking. I doubt that many other brands could have rebounded as quickly and as effectively from such a consequential marketing error.

Ignorance often leads to an incomplete analysis of the data available; the lack of a thorough investigation regarding the downstream impact of a decision and its likely scenarios can also drastically increase the risk of unexpected behavioral impacts by the marketplace or your direct clients. Worse, such fallacies may be due to overconfidence (e.g. in management's ability to understand a situation, leading to insufficient investigations into the potential outcomes) and overreliance (e.g. on your experience to guide future decisions, causing you to believe that you've "seen this, done that" and don't need to fully evaluate or assess each new situation). Ignorance may also characterize the habits of employees, who are expected to take purposeful action and may be neglected in terms of proper training, input, or expertise; "let's figure it out as we go" usually isn't an optimal everyday motto in the workspace.

Error

Error basically builds on ignorance, as aforementioned—especially during the planning or early stages of initiative. In 2008, Tata Motors began manufacturing a tiny car aptly called the Tata Nano. Projecting a price of as little as $2,000 for each vehicle, it became and was marketed as "the cheapest car in the world" to sell. Tata Motors expected the masses to begin raving for this car, especially in regions of the world where owning a car was considered an unaffordable luxury. Given plenty of coverage from Western media, the Tata Nano soon became a global phenomenon, just as its executive team expected.

Unfortunately there was another consequence that was completely unexpected but just as drastic, due to an erroneous marketing campaign.

Tata Motors marketed their Nano as "the cheapest", a characteristic that became synonymous with the car, rendering it cheap in quality as well as in its price-tag in the minds of potential customers. This was because the company failed to understand the mentality of what it hoped would be its biggest market: India. In India, cars were indeed considered a luxury—but this definition extended to entail that Indians wanted their cars (if they could afford a car) to be their status symbol. They would sacrifice other luxuries and even necessities if it meant that they could have a nicer car which would be emblematic of their prosperity or popularity. Therefore, Indians felt no special attraction to the Tata Nano which cost so little and which would thus invite ridicule from their friends and relatives. The Chairman of Tata Group, Ratan Tata, eventually confessed that the company's marketing strategy had been a horrible mistake.

What if they'd sold the Tata Nano with traits of affordability and convenience? What if they'd presented it as a luxurious micro-car that was created *for* the average driver *by* the average driver, a car as practical as it was valuable? What if it was just a cuter and more compact version that cost less explicitly due to its smaller stature and *not* due to lesser quality or luxury? Imagine what a difference a word can make.

In the years since, Tata Motors has sold a good number of Nanos but it has in no way achieved the forecasted production levels that the company's executives always yearned for. Instead of selling 20,000 cars per month, the company sold less than an average of 20,000 annually. The automobile's fate was to become yet another cheap car in a market already brimming with cheap cars. It never managed to retaliate and recover from its initial failed campaign.

Immediate Interest

When short-term interests and immediate gain override and undermine long-term goals and visions, the entire company's foundation faces the threat of erosion. This manifests in the ridiculous outcome of the fierce, long-standing competition between the Apple iPhone and the Samsung Galaxy as both brands race to showcase the most cutting-edge technology in what is perhaps the most famous duel in the consumer electronics industry.

Samsung Galaxy recently tripped and fell flat on its screen—exploding on the ground, if you want to get literal—during a recent lap in this race. In August 2016, Samsung launched its much-touted Galaxy Note 7, causing a great stir and fanfare throughout New York City. Their goal was to have their Note 7 out and available to the public before the iPhone 7 Plus was ready. They succeeded in that; Apple's iPhone 7 Plus emerged in September.

The Samsung team's victory was extremely short-lived, however, mirroring their short-sighted patience.

Almost immediately after the product was launched and shipped, users began reporting issues with the phone—some of them extremely dangerous, since the phones were reported to catch fire or even explode. Samsung's engineers weren't able to duplicate the issue; crunched for time, they blamed one supplier's faulty batteries, while Samsung just went ahead and shipped even more phones (with batteries from another supplier) to consumers. The replacements they sent out were no better, reportedly having the same explosive tendencies.

This resulted in a second recall. Ultimately, Samsung dramatically announced the cancellation of the Note 7 altogether. The company meanwhile has recalled more than 2.5 million devices worldwide.

The New York Times penned an analysis of the problem, citing Samsung's corporate culture as a catalyst.[x] Former employees have described a top-down culture that's militaristic and even suffocating, where executives make demands without understanding product technologies and giving their employees the liberty to voice their own suggestions or opinions. Samsung testers were even commanded to keep all communications offline to "avoid lawsuits and subpoenas". Did that extend to electronic record keeping, too? Managing such a technologically complex challenge would be nothing short of a nightmare. The pairing of miscommunications with unaligned goals and short-sighted, competitive-fueled vision is a surefire recipe for disaster.

These outcomes only blow up exponentially in a scenario where the entire organization becomes fixated on immediate interests.

As of the time of this chapter's writing, the root cause for Samsung's Note 7 suicidal tendencies has neither been found nor corrected. The impact, though, is as clear as glass and twice as sharp. It took only two days in early September for Samsung's stock to plummet 11%, dropping $22 billion in market value (even though initial estimates regarding the damage had projected $1 billion in losses). The recall alone will continue to cost hundreds of millions of dollars. The lingering question, of course, is how long will Samsung's fallout last? And, just as importantly, what are the long-term consequences? The company has already planned the release of a "safe, buyable" Galaxy S8, but they'll have their hands full trying to convince a skeptical public—especially one that might already be more than happy with, say, a Google Pixel.

It's a classic misstep of over-ambitious or uncalculating executives;

x   Chen, B.X., & Sang-Hun, C. (2016, October 11). Why Samsung Abandoned Its Galaxy Note 7 Flagship Phone. *The New York Times*. Retrieved from https://www.nytimes.com/2016/10/12/business/international/samsung-galaxy-note7-terminated.html?_r=1.

they become too immersed with the prospect and achievement of short-term results that they give no consideration for the downstream effects. Such quarterly-focused executive teams, goaded by short-term reward systems and strategizing for immediate gratification, exclude themselves from exploring or brainstorming for unforeseen consequences.

> *"Without refection, we go blindly on our way, creating more unintended consequences, and failing to achieve anything useful."*
>
> —Margaret J. Wheatley

The moral of how pursuing immediate interests can backfire was also illustrated by the 2012 "company improvements" by the Red Lobster restaurant chain. In an effort to lower their operating costs without harming in-store efficiency, the executive folks of Red Lobster decided that it would be a good move to eliminate the busboy position in their staff. They reasoned that fellow restaurant chain Chili's had done this as part of its strategy to restructure its staff, and had allegedly enjoyed $25 million in annual savings. Red Lobster executives went the extra mile by also demoting some of their servers to lower-paying positions ("service assistants") and demanded that the remaining servers take on four tables instead of three.

At the time of the announcement, several critics did warn that such a configuration would hurt company morale. Red Lobster's spokesperson Heidi Schauer countered this argument fiercely, stating that both customers and employees supported the plan. The executives paid no heed to the naysayers.

Less than a year after they'd launched their new policy, Red Lobster found itself struggling to rebound from the mess. The "improvement" boomeranged, actually slashing sales that had already been suffering in the old-fashioned sit-down chain restaurant industry. Employee morale was indeed at an all-time low for the company, customer complaints were on the rise, and the company simply found itself unable to maintain its quality service under the new demands. Red Lobster's environment morphed into an embodiment of the dreaded overworked and underpaid scenario.

Chris Muller, the Dean of Boston University's Hospitality School, had been one of those warning that worker morale would suffer. "If you don't like the people you're working with and for... it's going to show," he's said. Regarding the Red Lobster experiment, Muller adds: "No customer ever went to a restaurant saying, *I love it here! They have the lowest labor costs in town!*"[xi]

Basic Values

The fourth cause of unintended consequences—basic values—is synonymous with stubbornness. It's the reason that progress-obstructing phrases such as "it's just the way we've always done it" or "this is how we always do it, so stop asking questions" spew out of people's mouths. Left unchecked and unrevised, basic values are like manacles that keep you fettered to certain actions or prohibit other possible approaches, regardless of whether the long-term outcome is favorable or not.

Such chains often encircle employees at fast-food restaurant chains, where a tracking system is used to ensure speedy service via the drive-through section. These installed timers are hooked up to a pair of sensors and begin tracking time once a car drives up to the speaker; the stopwatch stops when the car departs from the drive-through window and leaves the sensor's range. The daily times are aggregated and reported to the district supervisor for approval.

A former Burger King employee noted how the company cheated

---

xi   Pedicini, S., & Sentinel, O. (2012, July 12). Red Lobster cuts costs with new system for waiters, cutting busboys. Retrieved from http://articles.orlandosentinel.com/2012-07-12/business/os-red-lobster-service-assistants-20120712_1_red-lobster-darden-restaurants-servers.

the clock without disturbing the tracking system—to the detriment of customer service. On days when the restaurant wasn't meeting the timeframe goal (typically a 3-minute time slot), the manager instructed the staff to have each car pull around to the front of the restaurant immediately after paying and to then wait there for their order. Rather than handing the food out of the window, the staff would deliver the order to the customers waiting out at the front parking lot.

The district supervisor saw that the restaurant was meeting the 3-minute timeframe and was pleased; focused only on those results and believing the process to be bulletproof, he had no idea that customers ended up waiting longer for their food.

This is a case of basic values causing blind spots, ensuing in the inability to evaluate options due to "sacred cows" or tradition. At Burger King, it may have resulted in nothing more dramatic than a bit of delay and a grouchier empty stomach (which, as we've seen, is enough to drive away business, leading to worse consequences for the company). In a more urgent or impactful sort of environment, such as a hospital's emergency room or an auto manufacturer's factory, blind spots created by "basic value protocol" can be extremely pricy in terms of money, time, and energy—and can even cost patients and clients their lives.

Self-Defeating Prophecy

In February 2009, the D.C. City Council decided to prohibit stores in Washington D.C.'s Ward 6 section from selling single cans of beer. Proponents of this policy argued that it would ward off troublemaking drunks who tended to swing into a store, buy a beer, and then loiter around the sidewalks as they drank and made a ruckus. This ban would work, stated Ward 6 Councilman Tommy Wells, arguing that H Street experienced a significant reduction in complaints and arrests related to public drinking, urination, and disorderly conflict after a similar ban.

Many managers of liquor stores and beer distributors in the Ward 6 region disagreed, prophesizing that the unfair policy would result in clients avoiding their stores and "going down two blocks" to get their desired quantity of beer.

The result? The ward-wide ban backfired in Ward 6, just as the store managers predicted. After the ban, arrests for open container violations increased from 260 to 389, with 63 arrests for public urination during the first six months of 2009 as opposed to 46 respective arrests during the first six months of 2008. Overall complaints more than doubled.

The Council had created the 2-pack, which did nothing to ward off alcohol-related disorderly conduct. The law also prohibited retailers from allowing customers to buy a mixed pack. Public drinking abounded and worsened, since now the drunkards came in groups of two or three to split the cost and quantity of the alcohol. In 2012, the Council considered banning the sale of 2- and 3-packs, following the "basic value" of alcohol prohibition.

If you need a reminder, just check out the prior chapter regarding the amendment that ignited the Prohibition era in the 1920–30s. We all know how well that went.

A self-defeating prophecy is the complementary opposite of the self-fulling prophecy; it prevents what it predicts as a desirable outcome, creating instead a negative unanticipated consequence. Sometimes this self-sabotage is the result of rebellion to the prediction; the "audience" of a prediction may exhibit behavior to try to falsify this prediction (whether through action or inaction). Other times, even working to make a premonition come true can backfire by inadvertent actions that carry their own weight. There are times when the actions taken to reap the benefits from opportunities and steer clear or risks can directly lead to said opportunities and risks to disappear; it's the same mentality that goes into play when a highly anticipated film ensues in poor reviews primarily because there was too much hype and therefore inflated expectations (the film may have triumphed as an "underdog" movie in another scenario), or the mentality that keeps voters at home and away from election polls when they they've heard that their choice is predicted to win or when they've been led to believe that their own actions won't make a difference, or the reason you stop for fast-food after committing yourself to healthy eating.

It's just as easy for bad judgment and self-defeating prophecies to emerge from within the company itself. Walmart CEO Doug McMillon had his employees' best interests at heart when he announced the boost of his store's minimum wage in 2015. His intentions were to improve morale and retain happy employees, especially in the face of recent literature berating Walmart for its low wages and overall wage inequality. The decision would affect 500,000 of Walmart's total 1.3 million employees.

Instead of creating warm and fuzzy feelings with employees, McMillon's decision created uproar among the hundreds of thousands of workers who didn't get a raise. Long-term employees expressed the greatest frustration, feeling neglected and upset after working for over ten years at Walmart and making just $12/hour while new employees were coming in with $10/hour. Veteran employees also felt that their wages or hours would be slashed to pay for the increased minimum wage of the new hires.

Organizations such as the Economic-Policy Institute have conducted studies that show how firms usually increases the wages of long-standing employees who are making $1–2 above the minimum wage as they simultaneously boost the minimum wage. From a number of standpoints, this seems only fair. Unfortunately for Walmart, they did not do this. Whether they deemed it unnecessary or expensive, this choice boomeranged right back at them. Predictably, social media exploded with comments from disenchanted workers, worsening Walmart's headache since the executives had been attempting to solve exactly this issue of low employee morale and high turnover. Walmart rushed to address the pay issues of long-term employees, with the total cost of this action estimated to be over $2.7 billion.

Unintended or Unanticipated?

Throughout this chapter, I've sought to illustrate the five catalysts of negative unintended consequences. Each story is meant to show how one mere move or choice or sacred cow can snowball to monumental proportions depending on the number and intensity of the factors involved. Returning to our very first example, let it suffice to say that since the Wells Fargo scandal ignited the rage and disappointment of Americans throughout the country, John Stumpf has resigned as CEO, forfeiting $41 million in stock awards. Four top executives were also publicly fined and fired in February 2017. The company's reputation has plummeted, rendering it the biggest bank to ever be unaccredited by the Better Business Bureau and plaguing it with class-action lawsuits. The Justice Department continues its criminal investigations.

Merriam-Webster defines the term *unanticipated* as something that is "unexpected" and unforeseen"; it defines the term *unintended* as "not planned as purpose or goal; not deliberate or intended". In his article "Unintended but not unanticipated consequences", Dr. Frank de Zwart seeks to distinguish between the two, exploring how *unanticipated* has been overtaken by *unintended* since Dr. Merton's respective publications in 1936.[xii] The question he poses is whether the decline of *unanticipated* as an adjective is due to our ability to better anticipate consequences—albeit ones we consciously know to be unpleasant or unwanted—or have we simply conflated both terms?

However you choose to term these consequences, it is essential to spend time trying to analyze and identify them proactively in order

xii   De Zwart, F. (2015, April 12). Unintended but not unanticipated consequences | SpringerLink. Retrieved from https://link.springer.com/article/10.1007%2Fs11186-015-9247-6.

to prevent—as much as possible—both types of consequences. Zwart created the following chart to help distinguish the various types of outcomes, illuminating how some consequences can in fact be both unintended *and un*anticipated.

	Intended	Unintended
Anticipated	A	B
Unanticipated		D

Categories B and D both may entail undesirable consequences, but Category D harbors the most dangerous type as it can be unintentional, undesirable, and unpredicted all at the same time. My interest is in helping you define and master the tools and best practices which would bring to light more of Category D's unanticipated and unintended consequences, with the goal of developing a robust decision-making ecosystem to exterminate such consequences. In the next chapters, we'll examine six ways that executives can seek to control the outcomes of their strategic decisions.

Section II:
SECURE: A Six-Step Strategy For Mitigating Unintended Consequences

4
The 1ˢᵗ Strategy: Slow Down the Decision Process

"Wisely, and slow. They stumble that run fast."
—William Shakespeare

A GOLIATH IN ITS INDUSTRY, THE COCA-COLA COMPANY has reigned as a global beverage corporation with a long history of successful products and acquisitions; the company is best known for its flagship product Coca-Cola, invented in 1886. Yet nearly a century after its founding, in the early 1980s, the Coca-Cola Company found its company shares slipping in response to its rival Pepsi Company's "Pepsi Challenge" taste test results and marketing campaign. In response, Coca-Cola Co. developed a new formula coke—dubbing it the New Coke—and invested heavily in extensive taste tests and market research. New Coke continuously seemed to beat both Pepsi and the original Coca-Cola beverages in taste tests. Armed with this indication that people preferred the taste of this new alchemy over that of alternative beverages, the company plowed forward in 1985 and announced that it was replacing its original flagship cola with New Coke.

What they hadn't foreseen, of course, was the massive backlash that this would elicit.

Pepsi Co. cleverly spun the announcement of New Coke as

Coca-Cola Co. fearing and admitting that their "classic" product was less amazing than Pepsi's beverages. This counterattack permeated the market. In less than three months from the new product's release, Coca-Cola Co. snatched back New Coke and rereleased its original formula.

Even the most invincible warriors and giants have their weak spots and can be felled: an Achilles heel or a Cyclops blind spot. Coca-Cola's size and history couldn't insulate it from the consequences of its mistakes. Fortunately the company's CEO at the time, Roberto Goizueta, was just the type of leader you'd expect to respond aptly to such challenges. Throughout his career, Goizueta had demonstrated that he was willing to take risks and make disruptive changes in the face of strategic improvements, and he did indeed build quite an impressive resume before and after the New Coke fiasco. While he'd had the best intentions—with the goal of the project being to promote New Coke as the premier cola beverage on the market—he quickly realized that it had been no more than a poorly executed product launch.

Size won't insulate your company from the hard work and risks involved when it comes to making strategic business decisions, but privately-held firms are particularly vulnerable for making hasty or last-minute decisions given that their leaders are typically more involved in the business's day-to-day operations. In his book *The E-Myth*, Michael E. Gerber describes the challenges faced by leaders of smaller firms who must learn to work *on* their business more than *in* their business. While *time and tide wait for no man*, you can certainly make better use of the time given to you...

#1: Opt for System 2.

Specifically, you can "harness" the future by regularly scheduling time to deal with strategic challenges and opportunities. In doing so, you will begin to protect yourself from the claustrophobic feeling that you're running out of time during the decision-making process. Sometimes it's comforting and simultaneously invigorating to remember that we each have just as many hours in a day as do presidents, CEOs, human rights activists, single parents, and every other individual from any walk of life and in any profession around the world. The choice of what do with those 1,440 minutes given to us daily is the choice that we independently make—consciously or subconsciously—every single day.

As an executive, the decision to begin the process of strategizing is something that you—*you,* more than anyone—should and can take well in advance of the required deadline, as much as possible. You have far more to gain than you have to lose; allotting time to thoroughly think through a decision before the deadline allows for the proper level of clear-headed discussion and deliberation.

Whatever you do, don't make the mistake of underestimating those key components of discussion and deliberation. In *Thinking: Fast and Slow,* psychologist and Nobel Prize winner Daniel Kahneman explains how there are two systems that drive the way we think and decide:

- **System 1,** which is characterized as fast, intuitive, and emotional behavior.

- **System 2,** which is defined as slower, more deliberate, and more logical behavior.

Successful executives often pride themselves in their ability to make quick decisions based on their experience; contrary to that popular sentiment, however, Kahneman proves why such judgments are much riskier and often wrong, given that System 1—basing judgments on a vast store of memories that are associated with strong emotions—makes decisions based on limited and emotionally-charged information. System 2, instead, encourages the slow process of forming judgments based on conscious thinking and the critical examination of evidence, simply by taking more time and deliberating over a decision more thoroughly. In the company context, using more of System 2 gives you the chance to correct potential mistakes and revise your decisions prior to implementing them.

If you think about it, System 1 is the easier route (Kahneman goes so far as to describe it as lazy); System 2 takes effort, which requires time and expends energy. Little wonder that so many executives—forever keeping busy and running out of time—default to System 1, unfortunately making that a habit even when it comes to more significant and strategic decisions. Mix the inclination towards System 1 with the claustrophobic feeling that your time's up, and—voila!—you've got a surefire recipe for brewing unintended consequences.

#2: Schedule time proactively, regularly, and specifically.

Let's start with some scary stats, shall we?

According to research conducted and publicized by the *Harvard Business Review* examining 187 companies, the average of time spent by the senior level executives in discussing and making strategic decisions rounded out to *less than three hours* per month.[xiii] Furthermore, it was estimated that as much as **80% of the senior executives' time was actually devoted to issues that accounted for less than 20% of the companies' long-term value** (talk about turning the Pareto Principle on its head!). One global financial service firm reported that the top executives literally spent more time each year selecting the company's holiday card than debating the bank's strategy for the African continent in which they'd made significant capital investments.

Where does the time go, indeed?

50% of top management admitted that their agenda was either exactly the same from meeting to meeting or ad hoc, with **less than**

---

xiii   Mankins, M. (2014, November 05). Stop Wasting Valuable Time. *Harvard Business Review*. Retrieved from https://hbr.org/2004/09/stop-wasting-valuable-time.

5% of the respondents saying that the company had a "rigorous and disciplined process for focusing top management's time on the most important issues". The responsibility of decision making is treated as a function that is external to the daily operation of the business. If you stop to think about that, it's mind-blowingly obvious how such a mentality can quickly make a business careen off its tracks, yet it's something that so many of us have entrenched in our own company cultures. Common symptoms include: urgent issues always preceding important ones, frustrated team members, unaddressed issues, sloppy decisions, and undermined performance due to slow execution or conflicting choices.

Marakon Associates teamed up with the Economist Intelligence Unit to survey 156 conglomerates worldwide, each with sales topping $1 billion. In a rallying cry to "stop making plans; start making decisions", their study revealed that most executives fail at strategic planning because they don't do it often enough or because they're primarily focused on individual business units.[xiv] 66% of the surveyed companies stated that planning was a periodic event, seen as a necessary evil before the annual budgeting and capital-approval process. Without the rigorous planning or productive debate essential for success, these executives consider the decision-making process to be disconnecting, frustrating, and even useless.

The solution is straightforward: **change the timing and the focus of the process.**

- **Schedule frequent meetings and make them a regular part** of your business operations routine. Remember that it's not time that's against you, per say; it's the *lack of time* you should be arming yourself against. If you schedule it, you'll treat it as a priority.

---

xiv   Mankins, M., & Steele, R. (2006). Stop Making Plans; Start Making Decisions. *The Harvard Business Review*. Retrieved from https://hbr.org/2006/01/stop-making-plans-start-making-decisions.

- **Follow through** on those meetings. Setting (and meeting!) specific milestones will ensure that you take full advantage of the time allotted to strategizing.

- **Bring the intervals closer together** (schedule the meetings more frequently) when dealing with and deciding upon the most important decisions. More time equals less pressure, but don't forget to actually use this time. Some executives schedule such meetings with the best of intentions, only to then rob themselves of this much-needed time by cancelling the meetings because they feel overwhelmed by the daily fires that are forever burning in the organization—and these, left unchecked, will become a ravaging wildfire.

#3: Make strategic *decisions*—not just strategic *discussions*.

Yes, we just touched on this. But it's important enough that it's worth reiterating. The strategic planning phase entails most of the most valuable hours which you pour into your business, and it's even more effective if you've got a team to provide you with the brainstorming and perspectives you need. Invite and welcome ideas from all corners and departments, encouraging a robust consideration for alternatives and scenarios. Remember that your decision is the butterfly that can clap its wings and ignite a tsunami over in logistics or in customer service. You'll be more effective at solving puzzles if you gather all the pieces first.

As impactful as this phase is, however, it must culminate in a decision in order to have any sort of meaning.

Self-proclaimed procrastinator Tim Urban shared a TED talk entitled "Inside the Mind of a Master Procrastinator", explaining that procrastination shows up in two forms in everyone's life: procrastination on short-term activities and procrastination on long-term activities. The key difference is that the short-term activities are time-bound; in other words, the negative consequences have a much lower emotional impact on people. Long-term activities are trickier because they have no hard timeframe; as such, they have a much greater negative impact on people because they revolve most commonly around important life choices and strategic decisions.

You can apply this directly to an executive in the business setting. Think of the short-term activities as the day-to-day, routine decisions that an executive must make as a response to an event:

- *How do we resolve this client's complaint?*

- *Do we hire a new VP?*

The long-term activities are strategic to the firm's future and may seem vaguer at first:

- *What new markets do we want to enter?*

- *What should our employment strategy be to deal with hiring millennials into our firm?*

This is particularly appropriate when we examine the content of strategic planning meetings. Usually the topics being considered don't have a concrete deadline by which a decision must be made. As such, executives can delay the decision to gain more insight or information. There are certainly times when opting for a bit more time to decide can greatly increase the quality of the outcome and lower the risk of unintended consequences. However, if executives fail to focus on the act of deciding and are purely procrastinating, they can easily fall into the trap of allowing too much time to pass in search of the missing facts. This can render their planning time ineffective by producing decisions that have suffered solely from the delay (often producing negative unintended consequences) or even a lack of decision-making altogether.

You've deliberated; now act deliberately.

Taking Care of Business...

Goizueta aptly helped Coca-Cola Co. bounce back from its slip-up by responding intelligently and quickly to negative feedback. This was largely made possible by an interesting and positive unintended consequence: Coca-Cola Co.'s consumers revealed that they valued the original formula more. This ultimately helped to revitalize the product's brand image, embodied in the brand's subsequent spike in interest—so much so, in fact, that it led to suspicions that New Coke had merely been a marketing ploy to generate more interest in the classic product. While I doubt that this was the case, the company should be lauded for bouncing back so quickly and effectively from such a huge bust.

Market researchers and journalists have since pointed out that Coca-Cola Co.'s critical error was in adopting an oversimplified and unrealistic perspective. Completely overlooking the fact that people don't make purchases based strictly on taste, Coca-Cola Co.'s executives assumed that the blind taste test results were sufficient enough to determine what people would buy. If they'd stopped to think it through more thoroughly, they would realize—as they certainly knew, if only subconsciously—that consumer behavior is influenced very heavily by brand loyalty, personal biases, and the perceived notions of others.

The problem isn't that Coca-Cola Co. didn't have access to information on consumer behavior; the problem is that they never stopped to consider it in their rush to counterattack the "Pepsi Challenge".

That's not to say that Goizueta and his team could not have successfully launched New Coke. They could have, had they focused on transforming an objectively delicious beverage into a desirable product that they could market more emotionally and powerfully. They would have had to work very diligently and thoughtfully to ensure that a market with significant brand preferences would respond positively to such a brash action. Unfortunately, it appears that they grasped one piece of "eureka" data, hyped it up, and risked their brand without considering the realities of their market. As a result, the product tanked. From a marketing perspective, this story is quintessential of what *not* to do.

Three Techniques for Slowing Down the Decision-Making Process:

- Opt for System 2 (Thinking Slow).

- Schedule time in advance (regularly and specifically for strategizing).

- Make strategic decisions, not just strategic discussions (follow through).

It's about working towards success, instead of just hoping for it.

Slowing down the decision process by opting for System 2, maintaining a regular and thorough pattern for discussing and deliberating over strategies and ideas, and following through on the decision consciously and deliberately is a definite best practice for reducing unintended consequences that may arise from executive decisions. Employing these three techniques will reduce time-induced stress, encourage clearer and more logical thinking, and produce more effective decisions in a more timely and appropriate manner. The fusion of these competing forces results in the reduction of downstream unintended consequences.

5
The 2nd Strategy: Expand Your Knowledge

"An investment in knowledge pays the best interest."
—Benjamin Franklin

AN ANNOUNCEMENT IN JANUARY 2000 BEGAN THE era of the infamous AOL-Time Warner merger, a $165 billion deal which would be closed one year later. At the time of the merger's decision, AOL (America Online) was an American market sweetheart and a dominant service provider with a huge valuation in the economy and great ambitions; Time Warner, entailing a wealth of content, reigned as a media powerhouse that hadn't quite made the online impact that it desired. Given this context, it seemed that AOL and Time Warner could complement each other very well.

Curiously enough, this merger panned out as arguably the worst merger in history.

Things began rolling downhill almost as soon as the merger was announced. One of the greatest issues cited has been the clash of the differing company cultures of these two media giants, with the two companies intolerant of each other's policies to the point that their interactions and transactions were clearly tainted by a mutual disrespect. The leaders of the corporations—Stephen Case of AOL and Gerald Levin of Time Warner—never effectively culti-vated the synergy that would allow them to align and collaborate.

A few months later, the dot com bubble burst and that economy slipped into a recession. And as always in times of trouble, whatever misunderstandings and resentments brewing beneath the surface automatically found their way to burst through the top. AOL took a goodwill write-off of nearly $99 billion in 2002, with a total value of their stock plummeting from $226 billion to roughly $20 billion. AOL's business model imploded in the landscape of a market that was rapidly shifting from dial-up internet to faster broadband.

While many variables played into this equation of failure, many experts have pointed out Levin's erroneous leadership in the face of a "transformative" deal that severely over-promised and under-delivered. Many questioned why he did not demand a collar agreement with AOL, which would have protected Time Warner from the significant fluctu-ations in the AOL stock's price between the initiation and completion of the merger. Levin announced his resignation in the autumn of 2001, officially stepping down a few months later in 2002.

"Knowledge is of no value unless you put it into practice."
—Anton Chekhov

Your Decision is as Good as Your Information

One of the most powerful things you can accomplish as a leader is to expand your knowledge base before making strategic decisions that serve as the catalysts for the employees' purposeful actions. In business, a knowledge base is not a static collection of information; on the con-trary, it is a highly dynamic resource. It demands constant inflow, input, and insights, as well as the diligent filtering of this intelligence. This is especially critical in light of Robert Merton's theory that two of the primary causes of unintended consequences are ignorance and error.

In the quest for knowledge, most executives realize that they have more sources of information than they originally assumed. Unfortunately, not everyone comes to this conclusion; fewer still will get into the trouble of harnessing this knowledge. Doing so, however, can result in the gain of valuable insight that can lead to far more informed decisions, strategic leadership, effective team-building, and purposeful action with ensuing success.

An optimal place to begin seeking knowledge is within the firm itself.

Accessing knowledge within the firm ...

In his book *The Fifth Discipline*, American systems scientist and MIT senior lecturer Peter Senge writes about how entire companies can become "learning organizations", given the appropriate leadership and culture. He has defined such an organization as a group of people who work collectively to enhance their capabilities with the mission of producing results which they really care about. Such organizations are characterized by a conceptual framework of systems thinking, individual and personal mastery, mental models which promote inquiry and trust, a shared vision, and team learning.

Within the business itself, you can have a wealth of pertinent knowledge at your fingertips, as your employees can serve as a powerful aid in contributing to executive knowledge and curbing unintended consequences. It is your duty, however, to effectively mine for this information; create opportunities to engage with the various levels and departments, as each element has something different to share. Including the appropriate supervisors, managers, and directors will improve buy-in and facilitate their ability to address the inevitable questions that will arise from employees as they in turn endeavor to deliver expected outcomes.

There is a natural balance, of course, between the need to expand executive knowledge and the risk of engaging too many people too soon in the decision-making process. Research also suggests that companies don't organically develop into learning organizations. It takes constant work and rigorous practice to cultivate such a company culture, yet it's the greatest investment you can make within your firm. Keep in mind that as firms grow, they tend to lose their capacity to learn as company structures and individual thinking therefore becomes rigid or is more easily overlooked. In such scenarios, it is easier for the company to succumb to blind spots and groupthink habits.

To begin strategizing against ignorance and error, it can be extremely helpful to first understand the current limitations of your organization and then identify where executives need more information and how you can conduct research. For simplicity's sake, we can classify these into three categories:

- What an organization **knows it knows.**

- What an organization **knows it doesn't know.**

- What an organization **does not know it does not know.**

The most insidious category is the third: what is known, in psychology, as **the illusion of explanatory depth.** This concept was explored further by Art Markman, a psychology and marketing professor at the University of Texas, in a *Harvard Business Review* article entitled "Do You Know What You Don't Know?"[xv] He describes how we all harbor these "explanatory gaps", especially about things we regularly use or take for granted—citing examples such as trying to explain in depth the function of an everyday object (a zipper or a toilet) or trying to define business buzzwords ("streamlining business practices", "bleeding edge", etc.)—which we must learn to recognize and acknowledge. You can certainly consider blind spots and groupthink as knowledge gaps in the business context.

Uncovering and filling these gaps, Markman argues, is a learning

---

xv   Markman, A. (2012, May 03). Do You Know What You Don't Know? *Harvard Business Review*. Retrieved from https://hbr.org/2012/05/discover-what-you-need-to-know.

opportunity—not a sign of weakness. An undiagnosed gap means that we don't fully understand a problem even though we believe that we do or we've simply overlooked the fact that we don't. You can identify areas of deficient knowledge by asking people to explain their rationale for what they (and possibly the organization) believe to be true. By exposing the underlying depth of knowledge behind a concept, you can test how well the concept is understood and how well it stands intellectual scrutiny. Markman's research has proven that one of the most effective ways to counter the illusion of explanatory depth is by engaging others in collaborative learning and working to transform the business into a dynamic learning organization.

> *"Real knowledge is to know the extent of one's ignorance."*
> —Confucius

Accessing knowledge beyond the firm ...

I've been a fierce proponent for the power of executive peer learning since my time as President of Delphi Connection Systems, where I realized how the experiences of executives outside my firm provided me with invaluable insight and knowledge that was otherwise unavailable to me within my firm. In his book *The Breakthrough Company: How Everyday Companies Become Extraordinary Performers,* leadership consultant and lecturer Keith McFarland researched over 7,000 companies and interviewed over 1,500 growth-company executives to identify the secret to sustainable growth. He ultimately identified nine key strategies used by these executives, including the practice of seeking external counsel—or, as he describes it, **"erecting scaffolding around your business"**.

McFarland cautions that there's always room for improvement and collaboration, no matter how good we are—or think we are. Surrounding our companies with scaffolds, and constantly working to improve and strengthen them, is a powerful investment. I've outlined the creation of scaffolds built around my company's own decision-making processes in my first book, *Critical Mass: The 10 Explosive Powers of CEO Peer Groups*; just so, collaborating with peer executives in your own industry and executives from outside your industry who have faced similar strategic choices will give you the competitive edge gained through the real-world knowledge of how their decisions played out for them. You needn't make as many mistakes if you can first learn from the mistakes of others. You can spend more time perfecting the wheel when you don't have to keep reinventing it.

When top executives cultivated the desire to have their decisions questioned by executives outside their firm in CEO Peer Groups®, their leadership develops a characteristic of openness to being questioned from inside their firms as well. McFarland's term for internal key executive peers is "**insultants**" (inside consultants). These are the people who are willing to question a firm's existing assumptions and ways of doing business. These are people who aren't afraid of tipping over sacred cows for the sake of improvement and progress. These are the folks who will "tell it like it is", which is exactly what's needed. In addition, you can reach out to specialized consultants who are armed with the experience and insight needed to expand your own knowledge and your organization's capabilities. These are all invaluable allies, especially in times of making strategic decisions.

The U.S. Small Business Administration actually warns business executives against relying too much on external expert advice when evaluating their choices, citing this as one of the numerous mistakes that are often made during the decision-making process. Indeed, executives have the tendency to place too much weight on the words of experts, sometimes overvaluing the information provided by others to the point that they negate their own gut feelings. It is essential to keep all opinions in perspective. Personally, I believe that companies should hire the most qualified consultants they can afford and have them work on very specific aspects of the decision—and to *not* abdicate to them the responsibility for the overall final strategic decision, as this is truly the senior leaders' responsibility.

"Your perspective is always limited by how much you know. Expand your knowledge and you will transform your mind."
—Bruce Upton

Knowledgeable Proactivity

Actively harnessing and managing knowledge is essential for your organization's success, and this success is threefold: by making learning routine, you cultivate a learning organization; in doing so, you stimulate cultural change and innovation; in turn, enriched knowledge and improved collaborations will facilitate your decision-making capabilities. Leveraging the knowledge and experience of managers and employees alike is a critical step in expanding your own knowledge and wisdom as a senior executive. Do not forget to look towards the executives beyond your organization as well; gaining greater insight and varied perspectives from other executives' experiences will broaden your own horizons, strengthen your strategic initiative, save you from common mistakes, and provide you with a wider base of knowledge.

Had Levin taken the time—and directed others to spend more time—to gather relevant information pertaining to the enormous decision of signing up for a deal with AOL, he may have avoided the corporate calamity. He might have received and heeded the advice to strategize much more thoughtfully with a long-term and risk-adverse mindset before diving headfirst into what appeared on the surface as a flawless deal. A sense of time pressure, massive uncertainty, untested assumptions, and huge up-front investments are common ingredients in a recipe for disaster. Down the road, Levin's resignation (reportedly influenced by other personal and professional issues, including the death of his son) and the divorce of the AOL-Time Warner merger were both inevitable.

Whether it was a clash of cultures, a misreading of the dot-com bubble, or the collapse of the business model that sought to blend old media and new media culture, a more thorough and knowledgeable exploration of the future of the deal and of the companies involved may have spared these two conglomerates billions of dollars, hundreds of layoffs, and a top-ranking place as a "here's what's not to do" case study in business schools across the nation.

6

The 3rd Strategy: Clarify the Desired Outcome

"Clarity affords focus."

—Thomas Leonard

OH, WHAT SOME OF US WOULDN'T GIVE FOR A TIME machine. For the most noble purposes, of course. Spending more time with the grandparents. Preventing the Holocaust. Convincing Pope Gregory IX that black cats are simply cats with dark fur and no metaphysical powers. Maybe even catching a live Elvis concert.

Apple Computer, though . . . I have a feeling that Apple would incorporate, among whatever other escapades they had in mind, a visit to the mid-1990s in order to rethink their most hyped-up, sadly scrapped Copland OS project.

It started in 1994, when Apple began developing the code-named "Copland OS"—the updated version of the good old classic Macintosh operating system—to become the (original) Mac OS 8 successor to their System 7 OS. The project continued during 1995, gaining more popularity and enthusiasm as they began referring to the system as System 8 and Mac OS 8. As the project gathered momentum and began barreling forward, there were basically two ways that it could go: the furious empire-building frenzy would result in the company's as-of-yet greatest success . . . or it would snowball until it would overwhelm itself and ultimately crash and burn.

As you may have already guessed, the latter happened. Here's why.

Apple's project began with *four* people who began the project with *three* simple objectives: protective memory, preemptive multitasking, and several new OS features. Before long, the project managers from different departments of the company started realizing the potential of the project and they wanted in. Suddenly Copland was brimming with incentives, becoming *the* project at Apple; getting your feature into that OS seemed a surefire strategy to job security and notoriety. Enter "feature creep", the tendency for product/project requirements to increase during development beyond the original forecasts.

Within a year, those four teammates had become *hundreds*.

New features were added more rapidly than they could ever be completed. The completion date reverted to "pending". Several key "release dates" were neglected. The first developmental release was fairly buggy. In 1996, CEO Gil Amelio put technology manager Ellen Hancock in charge as Chief Technology Officer in an attempt to realign the project. Hancock decided it was best to scrap Copland altogether and replace the project with a third-party system (NeXTSTEP) which would become the basis of Apple's new Mac OS. MAC OS 8 was finally released in 1997, followed by MAC OS 9 in 1999 and MAC OS X in 2001.

You could play devil's advocate here, saying that Copland's failure was a blessing in disguise. If it wasn't for Copland, Apple might not have purchased NeXT, Steve Jobs may not have returned to reorganize the company which he'd founded 20 years prior, and many of Copland's features wouldn't have appeared in other successful OSes later released by the company.

Or maybe all of those things *would* have happened—more quickly, more effectively, and more peacefully.

Feature creep was largely to blame. But feature creep itself crawled out from a black hole called poor planning, disguised as overly-ambitious goals. That's the kind of black hole that sucks time, energy, and money—and it just pulls you in deeper the longer you try to wrestle with it. As Hancock realized, sometimes it's best to just step away, take your losses, and start looking for some clarity.

Begin with the End in Mind

The third strategy for working towards eliminating unintended negative consequences is to define—very, very clearly—what your desired and expected outcome is. As Stephen Covey emphasizes in his book *The 7 Habits of Highly Effective People,* the most straightforward and effective way to get to the end is to simply begin with the end in mind. Envision what you want. Make it tangible in your head. All of the world's greatest pieces of architecture were built twice: first in the architect's mind and only then in real life. You might get lucky once or twice. But luck can't cut it forever.

Sustainable success is not an accident.

Not only do you have to be crystal-clear in your own vision, you have to effectively convey it to others as well. Their perception and understanding makes up the majority of the paint on the completed canvas of your project. If their "purposeful action" is aligned with your desired outcome, you're that much more likely to achieve it. Furthermore, this is 100% your obligation. If you're expecting your people to engage in purposeful action towards a stated goal, *it is your responsibility* to ensure that they fully comprehend your vision.

This is where many executives trip. Sometimes they blame their employees for failing to complete a project to their standards without stopping to realize that they have not successfully conveyed their standards, goals, or even vision. The employees do not inherently have the same command of the vision—and they certainly aren't in possession of crystal balls to make up for it, either. The executives have brainstormed their concepts for far longer; they've warmed to them, gotten used to them, understood them, and maybe even ruminated over the potential potholes and missteps along the way. They may have even grown tired of talking about these concepts before even investing the time and energy to communicate with their teams.

"If you don't know where you're going, any road will get you there."

—Lewis Carol

That should never be an excuse. As a part of any strategic initiative—to the extent possible, and granted that the information isn't confidential—executives would save every team member so much time, energy, and headache if they simply brought key members into the planning phase *sooner*. As an executive, you should open a discussion especially with line managers, supervisors, and project leads. First, this helps to keep channels of communication open and unobstructed. More heads can be better than one, especially when it comes to brainstorming. More like-minded heads, in instances where being "caught up" and "in sync" are critical, is even more beneficial and can give you a significant competitive edge.

Secondly, this technique provides you with a "sounding board" for your ideas, enabling your people to ask questions to test their understanding about the process, strategies, risks, and advantages attached to the proposed initiative. By engaging a wider—albeit limited—audience and testing out your ideas, you'll be given more valuable insights and will have the chance to re-think elements of the plan, reducing the chances of future hold-ups and problems (including employee frustrations that you—as their executive—haven't thought the plan through). Even though you always may need to do some "thinking on your feet", you certainly don't want employees feeling like you're making up the plan as you go along.

Naturally, you're going to have to be flexible; the future is fluid and never set in stone. That's all the more reason to invite a diversity of thoughts and views to the table; more perspectives can lead to a far more multi-dimensional picture of future projections that you might never have seen on your own. Additional information will help paint a much more vivid picture of what you expect to accomplish, giving everyone a much stronger sense for what the desired outcome will be and what must be done to achieve it. Don't fall into the trap of thinking you've got to have it "all figured out" before telling anyone. As much as possible, fight the desire to deliver a completed picture during the planning phase.

The "middlemen" of your business—i.e. mid-level managers and project leads—will also have much to gain from this, since they don't have to suffer in the unenviable position of trying to explain a strategy about which they know very little and for which they haven't shared any input and thus don't really care about. Don't put your messengers in the position where employees may try to shoot them down; arm them with essential information instead. The more effectively you've conveyed to them your message, the more capably they'll be able to convey it in turn.

Finally, sharing your strategy gives your people a sense of ownership over the idea. Who doesn't want to feel respected, acknowledged, and taken into account? That's basic human nature, and you can read any Dale Carnegie book for a plethora of examples (seriously recommended!). If they feel that it belongs to them as well, they'll be more inclined to care about it and spend time thinking over it. They'll be far more excited and committed to achieving it and achieving it brilliantly. And then, in turn, they will be fully qualified and capable of effectively translating a vision that is rich with details and no longer ambiguous.

Four Advantages of Clarity in the Planning Phase:

- Encourages communication.
- Provides a sounding board for ideas.

- Creates a multidimensional, more complete picture.
- Offers a sense of ownership.

"In the absence of clearly-defned goals, we become strangely loyal to performing daily trivia until ultimately we become enslaved by it."
—Robert A. Heinlein

The Trick to Staying on Track

I suppose that Apple's executives could have more wisely focused on delivering a minimum viable product (MVP) that met their initial agreed-to list of clearly-defined requirements, with the option of refining and adding features later on. In such a scenario, Copland may have had a better chance of launching successfully. But the company slipped into quicksand from the moment executives allowed their project managers to integrate a growing number of pet projects that made the initial objective progressively more difficult—and, finally, impossible—to meet.

That's not to say that those pet projects were frivolous or unsound. On the contrary, many of the technologies were outstanding ideas that did eventually find their place in subsequent OSes. When viewed in a different context, these ideas were extremely commendable—and that's likely the characteristic that made it so hard for executives to push them aside. But that is a piece of the puzzle of leadership: the ability to see the entire forest and not get lost in the trees. By focusing on the clearly defined goal—and *only* by this focus—would leadership stand a chance to make those tough decisions and say "no" to good ideas when needed.

Apple failed in that. Had they clearly defined the scope of the project from the very beginning and stuck to their guns by telling project managers "not now", and had they finished their original project on time and on budget, they could have easily presented Copland as a success. They may have easily rolled out new features in subsequent updates, developing them even more strategically and wisely based on customer feedback and market research. Instead, they sacrificed pragmatism in favor of misguided ambition.

That is what excellent leaders must look out for, after all. They must be able to recognize the tipping point when "one more good feature" becomes "too much", and ensure that they don't overstep the line. One tried and tested way to do so is to stay true to clearly defined objectives.

7

The 4ᵗʰ Strategy: Unify the Team

"Few things help an individual more than to place responsibility upon him, and to let him know that you trust him."

—Booker T. Washington

MICROMANAGEMENT IS A DANGEROUS LEADERSHIP policy. Case in point: Martha Stewart.

Once upon a time—just a few years ago—Martha Stewart was inarguably experiencing her professional days in the sun. She reigned as household name, with her brand synonymous with quality and style and an All-American wholesomeness. For countless of housewives and women across the nation, her word was the gospel regarding anything related to the home and garden. Escaping from what has been characterized as an angry, sullen household and working-class family roots in New Jersey, Stewart eventually quit her job as a stockbroker in the '70s to launch a catering business in Connecticut. Leveraging connections and building an impressive brand as an expert in elegant home entertaining, she soon moved on to create a sensational career.

In 1996, when she took her corporation Martha Stewart Living Omnimedia public, she commanded a net worth of over $1 billion and was one of the wealthiest businesswomen in America. By 2001, she was second only to Queen Elizabeth of England as the most written about woman in the world, with her name reportedly appearing more frequently in the news than any other woman except that of Hilary Clinton, the First Lady of the White House at the time.

Then word began trickling along the grapevine that Stewart wasn't a very good leader.

Stories emerged that she treated people poorly—her partners and (even more importantly) her subordinates. The media broadcasted anecdotes of pride, contempt, and arrogance; these began sprouting around like a fungal disease in the grapevine, gnawing at Stewart's fruitful success. In the decades following the corporation's public launch, America has been privy to Stewart's well-documented legal troubles, tumbling stock prices, and her shaky fall from the pedestal she'd fought so hard to perch upon.

Former executives began raising doubts and concerns, voicing their complaints anonymously to *Vanity Fair* in 2013. "Martha's an omnivore. She just wants more, more, more [...] it's her genius and it's in some ways her downfall—that 'always hungry' thing," one longtime executive shared. Another former CEO described Stewart as a "triangulator", pitting people against people who should have been collaborating, cultivating a culture of tension that she seemed to be comfortable with. Yet another cited her inability to delegate and trust: "The company should be more successful, but it is just limping along, because of her—because she doesn't trust anybody and she has to control everything. [She] is delightful, charming, brilliant, fascinating—if you are in the room alone with her. You bring a third person in and it becomes poisonous. She has to dominate."[xvi]

Surely the tainted corporate culture—with whatever level of

---

xvi   Martha Stewart's Legal Troubles and the Voracious Appetite for "More" That Friends Call Her Downfall. (2013, August). *Vanity Fair*. Retrieved from http://www.vanityfair.com/news/2013/08/martha-stewart-lawsuit-spending.

toxicity it truly entailed—took its toll on the company and the brand. Surely this also encompasses Stewart's approach to leadership: one that seemed to always defy delegation and collaboration. Stewart aligned herself with her company to the extent that the brand and the person became inseparable. Her story is that of the rise and fall of an empire, with a queen who ultimately reigned in the blame-game.

"The inability to delegate is one of the biggest problems I see with managers at all levels."
—Eli Broad

The Curse of Micromanagement

Martha Stewart's personality is what made her brand and empire possible in the first place; it would not be fair to suggest she had to change it. But her Achilles heel was her unwillingness to delegate, share, and collaborate: her inability to allow skilled individuals to do their jobs within her corporation. Former executives have cited her incapability to let go of control as a primary catalyst for the company's downfall. Shying away from accountability, she reportedly blamed her board for legal and financial troubles, ignoring the fact that she commanded over 80% of the voting shares and played a large part in assembling the board itself based on her personal preferences regarding personalities (e.g. including her celebrity hairdresser) instead of focusing on experts who could further empower and expand her company.

Former employees and insiders have suggested that their self-described "maniacal micromanager" leader had issues trusting her team. This naturally bred an environment of combativeness instead of cooperation. Stewart's attempts at micromanagement stem from a place of insecurity and fear—fear of failure, fear that other people can't do what you need or want them to do, or fear that they won't. This hurt the boardroom, with tangible results emerging in the form of executive turnover and poor financial performance. Had Stewart instead empowered her partners, board members, and teams to make decisions and collaborate amongst themselves, the fate of her company would have been quite different. They would have navigated through inevitable struggles more profitably and more devotedly.

Empirical evidence supports this theory in the form of moderate successes that occurred once it seemed Stewart had allowed others to implement strategies without her micromanaging domination. Perhaps not coincidentally, board shakeups around 2013 led to more profitable quarters. Scrap metal executive Daniel Dienst was appointed as CEO and credited with implementing cost-cutting measures that allowed MSLO to turn a profit even when revenues were down. In the summer of 2015, MSLO was sold for $353 million to Sequentail Brands Group, with Stewart remaining onboard as the Chief Creative Officer.

So how do we spot micromanagement? And how can we avoid it?

A **micromanager** is someone who dictates and triangulates. These people condemn their companies—albeit unwittingly—by their own attitudes. In an article for the *Harvard Business Review,* Berkeley professor of management Jenny Chatman argues that micromanagement typically has nothing to do with employee performance; instead she says, addressing employees, that "it's more about your bosses' level of internal anxiety and need to control situations more than anything about you."[xvii]

For your own sake, that of your team, and that of your entire company, it's essential to understand how micromanagement establishes mistrust and suffocates the culture of your company, making it impossible for it to breathe and flourish. Many of us understand the "common sense" of trusting our teams as being vital to the growth and success of an organization, but it can be an immense challenge when it comes to letting go of our "baby".

---

xvii   Gallo, A. (2011, September 22). Stop Being Micromanaged. *Harvard Business Review.* Retrieved from https://hbr.org/2011/09/stop-being-micromanaged.

As a capable and good leader, you must acknowledge that you don't have the bandwidth or the technical knowledge to do everything—and you shouldn't have to. The reason human societies have thrived for centuries is simply based on the fact that we are stronger, smarter, and better together. Our strengths complement one another to ensue in something far greater than ourselves. The trick is in learning to collaborate and interact *effectively* (i.e. successfully producing a desired or intended result). That is the alchemy for better interpersonal relations, which is a fundamental cornerstone of success.

> *"No person will make a great business who wants to do it all himself or get all the credit."*
> —Andrew Carnegie

When "Delegate and Collaborate" Transcends "Dictate and Triangulate"

Substituting or bypassing micromanagement for a leadership that is instead based on delegation and collaboration is the most effective managerial evolution you could ever hope to achieve. This is the fourth strategy that will protect you from unintended consequences. By practicing these two key managerial behaviors—**delegation** and **collaboration**—you instill a culture of trust, communication, insight, motivation, dedication, and progress, all of which fuse to form a collectively aware, aligned, and strategically intelligent learning organization.

The Art of Delegation

Merriam-Webster explains **delegation** as "the act of empowering to act for another".[xviii] The key word here is *empowering*. Delegation is an art that takes practice for true mastery—it is, after all, the act of

---

xviii   Delegation [Def. 1]. (n.d.) In *Merriam-Webster*. Retrieved from https://www.merriam-webster.com/dictionary/delegation.

persuading someone to do something at your bidding. You are getting someone to do something, ideally in a way that will provide you your desired results and ideally with this person's full agreement and aligned intentions. Delegation can be powerful and purposeful.

As a leader, **effective delegation serves you in multiple ways:**

- **Task and workload distribution.** Two heads are better than one, four hands are faster than two, and so forth.

- **Ability and skillset development (including decision-making).** Practice makes perfect, so make your people do the things they should or could be doing. Let the consultants consult. Let the team leaders lead. Let the accountants do their math. Let the publicists work on their articles.

- **A culture of trust and cooperation.** That's the basis of any positive relationship, whether personal or professional. More specifically, it's the hallmark of good parenting—a fitting metaphor, if you think of your project, department, or company as your "baby". Your "kids" should like you and respect you. They should understand you're in charge and they shouldn't try to undermine your authority, but on the other hand they should appreciate that you respect them and cherish them as fellow human beings in turn. If this mutual trust, appreciation, and cooperation exists, you've succeeded in harnessing the potential of organizational greatness. Your company can thrive and survive beyond you, just like a grown-up kid.

- **Shared alignment, better progress.** Shared authority should align with shared goals, which means mutual investment and "ownership" of a project or vision. This is the fast-track to propelling a project or company forward, since it means that all hands are on deck and nobody is acting as an anchor that tries to hold the ship back.

- **Freed time, prioritized focus, and the big-picture view.** By enabling your people to do all of the above, you free yourself of the need to do those tasks. Instead, you can focus on *your* job: strategic leadership. Whether you think of yourself as the movie director, the puppet-master, or the puzzle-solver of your firm, you are the one who has to ensure that all the pieces are aligned. While the other folks are focusing on the trees, you've got to oversee the entire forest (i.e. senior-level issues and activities). By delegating, you manage to keep your big-picture view, swooping in to put out a fire or realign a crooked forest path only when you must.

You and fellow senior executives should determine how to effectively delegate to your people by clearly communicating the expected outcome from the very beginning. Doing so is a matter of balance: you need to give your teams enough leeway and breathing space to accomplish the necessary tasks while simultaneously ensuring that lower-level employees don't overstep their responsibilities or take on more than they can handle. A very positive and relevant byproduct of effective delegation is that it helps to bring together the decision-making and the project-achieving areas; those who are closest to the action often have unique insight that will help you craft a strategy to achieve the desired outcome, therefore helping to mitigate unintended consequences.

It still isn't a crystal ball, but few things will bring you closer to a realistic projection of the future outcome.

The internationally acclaimed and ethics-oriented management consultancy Management Centre (=mc) has drawn up a guide to effective delegation, identifying **six levels of authority** that can be assigned when delegating in order to ensure that authorities are clearly communicated.[xix] At the various levels, here's how you would behave and delegate as a project manager speaking to your team or staff:

- **Level 1. You retain full control of the situation**: "Look into the problem and bring me information; I'll decide what to do about it."

- **Level 2. You hand over some responsibility and accept an exploration of options while retaining decision-making power**: "Look into the problem and let me know what alternatives exist, with their pros and cons, and what you'd recommend; then I'll let you know what to do."

- **Level 3. You hand over the responsibility of sorting through options but maintain the right to make the final call**: "Look into the problem and let me know what you are planning to do; don't take action until I agree."

- **Level 4. You offer others the authority to act and decide while requiring regular updates and retaining the power to intercede as you deem necessary**: "Look into the problem; let me know what you intend to do; do it unless I say 'no'."

- **Level 5. You delegate responsibility for the task and give the person the authority to act as necessary in order to achieve the goal; they still need to report to you**, as you are still ultimately accountable for the success or failure of the task: "Take action; let me know what you did."

- **Level 6. You are handing over responsibility and authority for the whole project**, placing full trust in this person. "Take action; no further contact with me is required."

Delegation is not without its risks. Especially concerning full

---

xix   *Effective Delegation* (Publication). (2012). Retrieved from http://www.managementcentre.co.uk/downloads/EffectiveDelegation.pdf.

delegation—at Level 6—you need to ensure that you are not simply abdicating responsibility for the sake of avoiding accountability. In each scenario, you must decide which level of authority is most appropriate in light of the situation and the person to whom you shall delegate. If you delegate at too high a level, you run the risk of setting people up for failure if they do not have the competence or skillset to succeed at the task. If you delegate at too low a level, you may be micromanaging; you will lose the potential of your team's talents and insights and effort, while they may also feel stifled or resentful. Finding this balance is the key to effective and timely delegation.

As with any decision, remember that there is always an inevitable degree of risk attached. Choosing the right level of delegation will help you sidestep the majority of the risks and reduce the potential for unintended consequences. Setting a clearly defined framework, with a clarified timeframe and an aligned goal, is essential to ensuring the task can be done both effectively and efficiently.

> *"When the cement is wet, you can move it with a trial; when it hardens, you need a jackhammer."*
> —Michael Houlihan

The Art of Collaboration

Just as important as delegation, however, is the art of **collaboration**: the action of working with someone.

A collaborative culture is evident in the ways that teams are built and in the executive's role within said teams. Although the senior executive must maintain accountability for the final outcome, creating a culture of collaboration is essential to the provision of a greater quantity and quality of input from the team. At the core of collaboration, you will discover a sense of shared purpose. Including people—beyond senior executives—in the research and the making of strategic decisions has a markedly mitigating effect on unintended consequences because it builds cooperation, alignment, excitement, and thus both insight and productivity.

Collaboration done right produces what Kellogg School of Management professor Leigh Thompson calls "**a creative conspiracy**". In her book, *Creative Conspiracy: The New Rules of Breakthrough Collaboration,* Thompson outlines the exact ways in which creative conspiracies—or the lack thereof—affect the success of any team in any organization.[xx] Some of her key tips include:

- **Give them purpose.** Left to their own devices, teams are less creative than individuals.

- **Boundaries enable focus.** Providing "rules" to teams actually increases inventiveness.

- **Encourage more input first.** Keep brainstorming before you dive into the specifics of an idea; at this stage, focus more on a *quantity* of ideas.

- **Embrace diversity and change.** Fluctuating membership enhances a team's innovation.

- **Understand the brainstorming process.** Most leaders cannot articulate the four basic rules of brainstorming, as Thompson cites from advertising executive and creativity theorist Alex F. Osborn (who coined "brainstorming"): go for quantity; withhold criticism; welcome wild ideas; combine and improve ideas.

Effective collaboration is likewise a balancing act. Too many cooks in the kitchen can create an overwhelming atmosphere that ensues in misunderstandings, frustrations, and unsavory food. Collaboration also takes time. It is not free. It can't be forced. And you don't have a guarantee of positive outcomes or concrete success, either.

---

xx   Thompson, L. L. (2013). *Creative conspiracy: the new rules of breakthrough collaboration.* Boston, MA: Harvard Business Review Press.

Senior executives can take steps to fortify their collaboration strategy by putting in place a system and set of processes that include a strict focus on execution and a focus on the results of the collaboration. Senior executives should still play a strong role as a leader; at some point, they will have to call for a decision and may even need to insist that it be made in order for the project to proceed. It is just as important, on the other hand, for them to allocate responsibilities and decision making to employees, encouraging meetings for collective brainstorming and debates.

The most distinct and powerful collaboration, however, takes place under certain conditions. Without the right variables, collaboration might be partial (working in parallel but not together) or even oppositional (i.e. sharing and leveraging information to grow a counterculture based on opposition and defense). Robert J. Thomas, the executive director of the Accenture Institute, explains that collaboration is most effective when people are tackling problems that are characterized by one or more of the following three elements[xxi]:

- The problem is not a routine or regular issue; there is no obvious solution.

- The problem-solving process lacks structure; there isn't a familiar road to follow.

- The problem requires collective volition, a negotiation of meaning and order; some sort of sharing is needed but cannot be mandated.

These three conditions are very common when senior executives seek to undertake strategic decisions. In such situations, calling for collaboration is more than appropriate; it is essential. Don't make strategic decisions within the wood-paneled vacuum of the C-suite if you hope to achieve your desired results. Much of that desired outcome is

xxi   Thomas, R. J. (2011, June 1). The Three Essential Ingredients of Great Collaborations. *Harvard Business Review*. Retrieved from https://hbr.org/2011/06/the-three-essential-ingredient.

dependent on the purposeful action of the larger organization; gaining their involvement, trust, and help—as early as possible—can only aid in a better implementation of effort.

There is, of course, a time for welcoming people into the planning process. There is likewise a place; it is your job to also identify the areas where input is appropriate and needed. Finally, there is the matter of the *process* of involvement, the "how" that complements the aforementioned "when" and "where" and "who". You can base this on the **three fundamental rules of effective collaboration:**

- **Be prepared to explain "why".** People are more likely to work with you if you get them on your side, and the most powerful way is to ensure that you share a goal. They need to understand that they are vital to the desired outcome of the strategy. Confiding in them breeds trust and transparency and provides a sense of camaraderie and honesty. By taking the time and effort to explain to them why they are being asked to do something—how they are significant and fit in the larger picture—helps them feel happier and more motivated. That enthusiasm is directly infused in the project and overall corporate culture, creating an environment optimal for progress and sustainable success.

- **Encourage dissent.** Allowing creativity and innovation means letting employees feel comfortable disagreeing with each other and with senior executives without the fear of retribution or rebuttal. They have to be willing to try new things and toss out fresh ideas. Reward employees who are able to fight for their ideas without getting into fights over their ideas; this empowers them to contribute and take on ownership for the outcome, further improving the process and the team spirit.

- **Be prepared to make the final call and then act upon it.** Senior executives must retain the responsibility and willingness to make the final decision. It is their duty to prevent the team from revisiting the decision once it has been decided upon so that the team isn't chasing its tail in circles. Enough time should be allotted to evaluate options, hear and absorb everyone's arguments, and filter through this input to make the ultimate choice. While it's essential to clearly and patiently articulate the reasoning for this decision, it is just as important to help the team then move on by focusing on the next step: purposeful action as required to achieve the stated outcome.

Six Levels of Delegation:

1. Look into the problem; report to me; I'll decide what to do.
2. Look into the problem; let me know of alternative actions; recommend one for my approval.
3. Look into the problem; let me know what you want to do; don't take action until I approve.
4. Look into the problem; let me know what you intend to do; do it unless I say "no".
5. Take action; let me know what you did.
6. Take action; no further contact with me is required.

Three Rules of Collaboration:

1. Explain "why".
2. Encourage dissent and creativity.
3. Be prepared to make the final decision and act upon it.

"Don't be a bottleneck. If a matter is not a decision for the President or you, delegate it. Force responsibility down and

out. Find problem areas, add structure and delegate. The
pressure is to do the reverse. Resist it."
—Donald Rumsfeld (21st U.S. Secretary of Defense)

The Magic Beyond the C-suite

A micromanaging leader isn't necessarily a selfish or a tyrannical one, mind you—not intentionally, anyway. Jimmy Carter has been hailed by many as one of the most pure-hearted and emotionally intelligent presidents to ever reside in the White House. That didn't stop him from earning a bad rap as a president, however, due to his micromanagement tendencies, which some experts cite to explain his single term in office. He's been accused of an inability to delegate; lamenting over a bombardment of decision papers, he decided to take a course in speed-reading instead of reorganizing his staff to help share and streamline the process. Such stories are plentiful in his annotated journals—published as *White House Diary*—which chronicled his time at the Oval Office. The former president has confessed: "I was sometimes accused of 'micromanaging' the affairs of government and being excessively autocratic, and I must admit that my critics probably had a valid point."[xxii]

Remember that sustainable success isn't accidental. Martha Stewart's passion and dedication for what she did was obvious (and still is) and her great achievements should be chalked up to hard work and good market judgment as well as good timing, given that her "entertainment guru" persona aligned perfectly with the maturation and affluence of the baby boomer market. But like every warrior, she had an Achilles heel; that's the sort of thing that can cause even the greatest leaders to limp and stumble if it's not checked out quickly enough. Stewart realized, eventually, that micromanagers create macro problems. She's been commendably fighting to get back on her feet ever since.

---

xxii   Plant, C. (2012, June 20). Jimmy Carter – The Micro-Manager as a Leader. Retrieved from http://materialminds.com/leadership-development/leaders/jimmy-carter-the-micro-manager-as-a-leader/.

The C-suite—the group of a corporation's most important senior executives—will discover the magic if they dare to venture outside of their comfort zone of that wood-paneled vacuum (or however it is internally decorated). Members of this group carry on their shoulders the weight of high-stakes decisions, a demanding workload, and all of the entailed accountability and stress. The best of them, however, still see beyond themselves. They know that they have the opportunity to gain fresh insights, increased effort, shared ownership, and the cultivation of a healthy corporate culture if they effective delegate and collaborate with peers and employees beyond the C-suite. This is especially important in the struggle to mitigate unintended consequences, since those within the company now experience an entirely new level of ownership and understanding for the desired outcome.

Whether you're the head of a small family firm or the leader of the free world, these internal connections and alliances are priceless.

——— 8 ———
The 5th Strategy: Retain Control

"Control your own destiny, or someone else will."
—Jack Welch

"IT WAS JUST A MATTER OF TIME, AND YET KODAK DIDN'T really embrace any of it. That camera never saw the light of day."

These words came from the mouth of Steve Sasson, inventor of the digital camera (referred to in the above quote) and former engineer of Kodak—which at the time dominated 90% of domestic film sales and 85% of domestic camera, and would reign in the 1990s as one of the world's most five valuable brands.[xxiii] Sasson approached his bosses in 1975 with this invention of the first digital camera. Instead of soaring over the moon with the news of such an incredibly innovative break-through, his seniors shot down and ridiculed Sasson's idea in a fervent attempt to downplay technology and, in essence, future advancements.

The day came, of course, when the consequences boomeranged back to bite them.

"A capitalist will sell you the rope to hang him," Vladimir Lenin is said to have sneered. Not necessarily, I think, unless we're looking at an executive or entrepreneur who errs on the side of short-sighted

---

xxiii   The last Kodak moment? (2012, January 14). *The Economist*. Retrieved from http://www.economist.com/node/21542796.

vision (which is ironic, when you consider that strategic planning and visionary goals are cornerstones of successful entrepreneurship, but true). A hundred years after its founding in 1880, Kodak had established an empire for itself, bolstered by brilliant branding ("Kodak moment", anyone?) and innovative technology. Yet even this king of the filming industry wasn't immune to failure. Unwilling to change, Kodak found itself slipping from its high ranking in the 1990s, with its descent morphing into a full-blown downward spiral that resulted in bankruptcy in 2012.

That's the deepest cut that wounded Kodak and knocked it off its throne: not the *incapability* of the senior executives to master this new frontier—the company practically invented the technology in-house and had research (by the famed Vince Barabba) suggesting that digital had the capability to replace film—but their *unwillingness*. The digital market appeared as an inevitable future that Kodak refused to acknowledge. By then refusing to embrace the change effectively and quickly enough, they failed to make a timely transition to digital. Had they leveraged their many advantages to get a head start in the digital frontier, Kodak may have been a leading household name to this day.

Time and tide wait for no man, as the old saying goes. Let's add technology as a third item on that list.

> *"As a leader, your every action has a consequence; make sure it is one you intend."*
> —Katherine Bryant

Set for Success: The Proactive Leader

Every "recipe" for sustainable success, regardless of market or industry, begins with clean culinary tools, a tried-and-tested oven or stove-top, and enough time on your side; in a word: **proactivity.** The Systems Sciences Institute of IBM has reported that "the cost to fix an error found after a software product was deployed was up to 100 times more than [that of] an error (bug) discovered during design." This same exact rationale can be applied to your strategic decisions. When errors are uncovered during the planning stages, you have the lenience of time to respond quickly and effectively. Unlike reactive behavior, proactivity can save you loads of money, time, energy, and frustration in the long run.

This can apply to nearly any situation in life. For a particularly potent example, you don't have to look further than the balance of life and death, as witnessed daily by doctors and nurses around the world. A proactive test and early diagnosis of a disease can literally mean the difference between a patient's recovery and an engraved R.I.P. on a tombstone.

Proactivity is accomplished when you gain more control over the implementation prior to—and during the early stages of—a strategic decision's implementation. You will drastically minimize negative downstream outcomes if you have the support of your staff to help you in this, especially if they demonstrate a willingness to admit mistakes or unexpected outcomes at the earliest stages of implementation. You must be open to hearing truths especially from the employees who have been charged with taking the purposeful action needed to achieve the desired outcome of the strategic decision.

Here are four straightforward **best practices that enable you to gain more control:**

1.   Conduct limited trials and simulations.

2.   Engage the employees closest to the action and solicit their unbiased feedback.

3.   Closely monitor the early stages of the strategic decision's implementation.

4.   Maintain a positive attitude.

Trials and Simulations (The Test Drive)

Congratulations are in order. You've brainstormed beyond the C-suite, you've gotten the company onboard, you've cultivated a learning organization, and you have a pretty good idea of what you're doing. All of your business assumptions and calculations have been completed with great care and proper precision. You're now ready to launch into the implementation of your strategic decision.

Everything still won't run like clockwork. I need you to expect that.

As soon as implementation of the decision begins, look for early signs of deviations from your planned assumptions. You can do so simply by setting up controlled trials and simulations that can expose these deviances to senior executives without damaging the larger employee population's morale or the firm's reputation in the marketplace. The goal of these trials is to reduce the uncertainty that manifests as unintended consequences at the time of full implementation. A well-constructed trial is like a microcosm of the projected future, testing the elements of the plan and their combinations in the real world.

Would you buy a car without going for a test drive? Would you apply to a university or job without doing any research about the organization? Would you ever buy a house without checking it out first? Would you ever ask someone to marry you without dating that person first? Would you move a chess piece during a world tournament without first thinking through your options?

Hopefully you answered "no" to the above questions. If you did, you're on the right track. Simply apply that same thinking to your business moves.

Senior executives must carefully select how the trials are to be completed and by whom. As always, it's a game of balance: seek to empower employees to run the trials but be crystal-clear to clarify the mission. Be careful not to "telegraph" that you expect your desired or predicted outcome and *only that*. Instead, help them understand that you and the team must seek to find all realistic outcomes of the decision and that you are open to anything they may discover. The goal is to simulate, as accurately as possibly, what will happen once the strategic decision is in full effect.

At the same time, you may wish to assign a second team to carry out unbiased surveys or studies to ensure that you have a solid grasp on the realities of the trials. Encourage them to conduct research designed to further test the work done by the first team that's running the trials. This can only contribute to your collection of real-world information, and this increase of input will enable you to take more informed actions.

Will you find unpleasant or till-then unexpected consequences? I certainly hope so. Scouting out for possible pitfalls at this early stage is what will enable you to avoid the landmines further down the road.

Employee Engagement (All Hands on Deck!)

Once you've completed trials and simulations, and have adjusted your approach accordingly to avoid any projected negative outcomes, your work is far from done. Even the best constructed trial may not be able to completely simulate the realities of full implementation, as we cannot guard against changing or new variables brought in by external forces. This is exactly why it is essential to keep your employees in the loop—specifically, those who are charged with the purposeful action to carry out the decision. Here, again, proactivity will serve you greatly: having a clear communication plan prepared in advance will help you to effectively bring your employees onboard by ensuring that they understand how your adjusted strategy will lead to success.

This is typically the point where senior executives begin to tire. And, sure, it takes effort and time to communicate the plan to those who haven't yet been as involved or invested. Your employees do not have the comfort of the context you've developed over time in formulating the plan. Uninformed, they do not—cannot—share your vision or your passion. Without a sense of ownership and purpose, there can be no commitment.

And that, my friend, can be lethal.

Once the captain falls asleep at the wheel—especially one who arrogantly refuses for anyone's help and demands to play the role of lookout, navigator, and steersman all alone—it's easy for the ship to hit an iceberg or capsize from the waves.

Take nothing for granted in your engagement with these employees. Do not allow yourself to succumb to tiredness or ignorance. To make things easier for all of you, you can have a template already set up with the tools developed and the information that can be shared with them to answer the variety of inevitable questions that will arise from folks who aren't as familiar with a project or process as you are. Take them under your wing and guide them. They are the frontline team who will be operationalizing the plan, and they *cannot* do it without a full appreciation and understanding for the process that has gotten you to this point.

This is an extremely critical time for the success of your strategy.

It is during this transition that many strategic decisions become infected with the germs of future unintended consequences, much like the rats that suddenly infest a ship. Having attained the understanding and appreciation is not enough, however. Sometimes to avoid projected storms or dangers, you must navigate the ship to new or even uncharted waters. This can be jarring or frightening to employees who are not aware of the background or context that has led you to make this decision to take this action. Keep them in the loop; help them so that they can help you.

In other words, this is not the time to "set it and forget it"—it's not the time to leave your food in the slow cooker; the waters and oils are boiling and bubbling, and you've got to be on standby if you value the existence of your kitchen. The senior executives must be personally involved to demonstrate both a level of competence to make the proper decision as well as the confidence to be willing to stand behind it. The larger employee population is depending on it. Even as the work is being transferred to your frontline team, you've got to remain at the ready to jump in to put out potential fires.

> *"The proactive approach to a mistake is to acknowledge it instantly, correct, and learn from it."*
> —Stephen Covey

Early Monitoring (Am I Doing This Right?)

By now, you've transferred the strategic plan on to the employees, whose effective performance correlates directly to the belief that their efforts will lead to the stated outcome of the strategic decision. Senior executive attention must now turn to monitoring the early results. It's the equivalent, so to speak, of sneaking in some sips or bites of the food that you're cooking to ensure that you're doing it right and to check if you need to add more of any certain ingredient.

Take care, again, that you don't cross the line from monitoring to micromanaging. Don't seize the ladle and push the team away. The employees should be armed with the insight and practice (thanks to their senior leaders) to now be fully capable of implementing the decision. Much like soccer coaches at a game, senior executives should root from the sidelines now as they watch their teams compete to score goals against other sports teams. These coaches have the obligation to stay alert and knowledgeable about the game's progress and the team members' status, and to provide input and encouragement when necessary without initiating unnecessary inferences or interferences.

Many a tide in a game has turned thanks to a coach's quick and insightful response to an unexpected outcome, injury, or mistake. Just so, senior executives must look for the early signs of problems in order to swiftly initiate corrective action—for it's about exercising control, when needed. Make it clear to your teams that your response to problems relies on them, too; your guidance won't be of much help if you don't receive timely or honest information.

Positivity

The best tool with which to arm yourself against the unexpected bumps in the road and the tsunamis of the sea is your attitude. Regardless of what unintended consequences may arise from your plan despite every attempt to mitigate them, your health (and that of your plan and your firm) is supported by your ability to maintain a positive attitude despite the odds. We should all be able to attest to this at a personal level as well as a professional one. Stanford University's Emma Seppala and University of Michigan's Kim Cameron contributed with proof that positivity works. "Too many companies bet on cut-throat, high-pressure, take-no-prisoners culture to drive their financial success," Seppala and Cameron argue.[xxiv] A growing body of research on positive organization psychology, however, points in the opposite direction; their findings include the following intriguing facts:

1. Healthcare expenditures at high-pressure companies are nearly 50% greater than at other organizations.

2. It's estimated that 80% of workplace accidents and over 80% of doctor visits are attributed to stress; studies have shown a strong link between negative leadership behavior and increased heart disease in employees.

3. Other studies showed that disengaged workers have 37% higher absenteeism, 49% more accidents, 60% more errors and defects, with the respective organization experiencing 18% lower productivity, 16% lower

---

xxiv   Cameron, K. & Seppalla, E. (2015, December 01). Proof That Positive Work Cultures Are More Productive. *Harvard Business Review.* Retrieved from https://hbr.org/2015/12/proof-that-positive-work-cultures-are-more-productive.

profitability, 37% lower job growth, 65% lower share price over time.

4. Businesses with highly engaged employees enjoyed 100% more job applications.

5. Workplace stress leads to an increase of nearly 50% in voluntary turnover, while replacing a single employee costs approximately 20% of that employee's salary.

Senior executives in particular contribute significantly to the company culture, including its collective approach to problem-solving. Building a company characterized by a positive attitude will enable your employees to face the challenges inherent in all strategic decisions and help you all together to mitigate the potential for unintended consequences.

To nurture a culture of positivity, here's a four-step strategy that can apply anywhere:

- **Foster social connections**. A large number of empirical studies confirm that positive social connections at work produce highly desirable results. It's human nature to gravitate towards where you feel comfortable and are appreciated and welcomed. There's a world of difference between getting up and dreading to go to work each day and facing *those people*, versus waking up and looking forward to a safe, interesting, and wonderful environment. Happy employees get sick less often, recover twice as fast from surgery, have a lower risk of being depressed, learn faster and remember longer, and perform better on the job.

- **Empathize**. As a boss, you have a huge impact on the cultivation of the company culture and on the moods of your employees. Every day is a choice: you can spread joy and excitement or you can spread panic and frustration. It's everyone's choice, of course, but you're in a position of influence;

your attitude will be noticed, mimicked, and absorbed far more quickly and easily. Jane Dutton and her colleagues at the Compassion Lab at the University of Michigan suggest that leaders who demonstrate compassion towards their employees foster individual and collective resilience in challenging times. It makes sense; most folks would take a bullet (albeit metaphorically) for a family member more naturally than they would for a stranger.

- **Go out of your way to help.** Daan Van Knippenberg of the Rotterdam School of Management shows that employees of self-sacrificing leaders are more cooperative (and thus productive) simply because they trust their leaders more. They are also more inclined to exhibit similar behavior (it goes for all of us: monkey see, monkey do!).

- **Encourage people to talk to you.** Research by Harvard's Amy Edmondson demonstrates that a culture of safety—in which leaders are inclusive, humble, kind, and encourage their staff to speak up and ask for help—leads to better learning and performance outcomes.[xxv]

"A pessimist sees the difficulty in every opportunity; an optimist sees the opportunity in every difficulty."
—Winston Churchill

Don't Let Your Kodak Moment Fade Away...

Kodak's executives feared that the digital element would cannibalize their very profitable film business; they chose, therefore, compliancy—never a wise move in an innovative society. We can consider the

---

xxv   Lee, F., Edmondson, A., Thomke, S., & Worline, M. (2004, June 01). The Mixed Effects of Inconsistency on Experimentation in Organizations (Doctoral dissertation, University of Michigan, 2004) [Abstract]. *Organization Science*, 310-326. Retrieved from http://dx.doi.org/10.1287/orsc.1040.0076.

Advantix Preview film and camera system as a decent microcosm to showcase Kodak's failed approach to digital technology. The Advantix hit the market in 1996 and was $500+ million project with a feature that allowed users to use the digital image to preview pictures they wished to print (a digital camera focused on print and film). Kodak's competitors hit the ground running in the digital frontier. By the time Kodak resigned itself to the truth of the market and made a concerted effort to delve in, it was too late. Smartphones and tablets had emerged as the newest innovations and next worthy successors.

Good leaders must be able to know when to take control of a situation by responding appropriately to market changes. Kodak was uniquely positioned to make a breakthrough push into the digital frontier based on the potential indicated by their 1981 research; had they done so, they would have had a far greater opportunity to create their circumstances rather than sitting back and letting the circumstances mold their fate instead. Successful leaders do not cling to outdated views or reactive behaviors; they realize that short-sighted visions can have dire results and unintended consequences that they may never be able to recover from.

Before, during, and after implementation of any strategic decision, you and your senior executives must stay actively involved and alert. Practice proactivity by conducting trials and simulations before full implementation. Engage your employees and solicit their unbiased feedback. Monitor and mentor your teams during the early stages of implementation. Throughout it all, remember that your attitude has the ability to move mountains.

By being inclusive, communicative, transparent, and collectively educated, you and your team have the greatest chance of avoiding unintended consequences and controlling ever-shifting situations within and beyond both your company and your market.

9

The 6th Strategy: Ensure You Stay Outcome Focused

"One way to boost our willpower and focus is to manage our distractions instead of letting them manage us."
—Daniel Goldman

THE EXECUTIVES OVER AT GREEN MOUNTAIN Coffee Roasters were over the moon about their brainchild, the one that would help the company defend its market share in a period of competitive turmoil. The year was 2014, and Green Mountain was tired of losing patents on its coffee pod designs. *Why not build technology into our Keurig 2.0 brewers?* the senior executives mused. *Why not force our consumers to buy coffee pods only from us?* It sounded like a good idea at the time so they snatched it up and hurled it out at the market. Because why not?

Why not, indeed: a good question—and one to which they should have paid quite a bit more attention.

Keurig's 2.0 brewer was purposefully constructed to be incompatible with the older reusable K-cup models which the company had become well known for, thus disallowing the use of third-party cups. Given its then-solid business model (selling the brewers and then the very profitable coffee pods) and its strong brand,

Green Mountain believed that loyal customers would embrace its new brewer without question. Excited at the prospect of an increased market share, CEO Brian Kelley called the venture "by far the largest and most significant product launch we've ever accomplished."[xxvi]

It may have been the largest, yes. Significant, too, if you're referring to the backlash in response to the new technology.

"My K-cup" had once reigned as an inexpensive option that allowed for more choices, since it could hold the coffee grounds of any coffee brand off the shelf. Eliminating it brought a surge of frustrations and furious complaints from customers who felt cheated and limited. In 2015, nearly half of the product's reviews on Amazon were 1-star ratings, with unhappy customers lashing out against the company and warning other prospective buyers to steer away. As one Amazon reviewer so eloquently put it: "If you don't mind zip-tying your hands behind your back when browsing your grocery store for K-Cups, then the 2.0 is the one for you. Feel like supporting Keurig's tactical attempt to increase the price of these little coffee pods? Or maybe you just need Keurig to lighten your wallet every week? Enjoy your new and unimproved brewer that does less for more of your money."[xxvii]

Competitors were quick to step up their game and step in, introducing hacks that would work around Keurig's restrictive technology. In November 2014, The Rogers Family Company cleverly supplied what customers demanded while plucking an emotional nerve. As a self-proclaimed "coffee liberator", their available-for-a-limited-time-only Freedom Clips—simple devices that allowed

xxvi   Peterson, H. (2015, May 06). Keurig's newest coffee machine has failed to take off. *Business Insider.* Retrieved from http://www.businessinsider.com/keurig-20-is-hurting-sales-2015-5.

xxvii   Peterson, H. (2015, May 07). It's official: Customers hate Keurig's newest coffee machine. *Business Insider.* Retrieved from http://www.businessinsider.sg/keurig-20-is-hurting-sales-2015-5/#G8HARRFfW1gUrxG9.97.

people to brew any sort of coffee with a Keurig brewer—became a major hit, fiercely marketed with the patriotic slogan of "Our Gift To You and Everyone . . . Freedom of Choice".[xxviii]

Meanwhile in the Keurig empire, the sky was falling. The second quarter of 2015 saw a 23% decline in brewer and accessory sales. Green Mountain struggled to regain its foothold, realizing the failure of its unpopular enforcement scheme. The company had lost its focus and its way—and thus its once-loyal following. "Quite honestly," admitted CEO Brian Kelly, "we're wrong. We shouldn't have taken [My K-cup] away. We're bringing it back."[xxix]

"People think focus means saying yes to the thing you've got to focus on. But that's not what it means at all. It means saying no to the hundred other good ideas that there are. You have to pick carefully."

—Steve Jobs

The Dangers of Getting Derailed

Removing your eyes from the prize means that you no longer see where you're going, greatly increasing the chances of tripping—possibly the precursor to a complete meltdown or downfall. Instead of maintaining their eyes on the prize (i.e. customer satisfaction), Keurig's executives were instead distracted by fears concerning their market share. While this is a reasonable fear which they did well to look into, they impulsively jumped on the first "solution" and lost their focus on what was most important for the brand. Retaining customer satisfaction would have minimized the risk of losing any market share, but the company

---

xxviii   The Freedom Clip. http://www.rogersfamilyco.com/index.php/freedom-clip/.

xxix   Hern, A. (2015, May 11). Keurig takes steps towards abandoning coffee-pod DRM. *The Guardian*. Retrieved from https://www.theguardian.com/technology/2015/may/11/keurig-takes-steps-towards-abandoning-coffee-pod-drm.

ignored that fact in an attempt to lock their customers into Keurig-branded pods, choosing to opt for poorly executed brute force.

The market's outraged reaction should have come as no surprise, and Keurig paid the price.

Good leaders must be attuned to their entire market and their customers' preferences. They need to regularly remind themselves and their teams that, at the end of the day, businesses exist to meet customer needs. Any decision to knowingly remove desirable features from a product must be very carefully considered, as such an action could prove extremely short-sighted—as in the case of Keurig.

Maintaining your focus is easier said than done—otherwise, everybody would be doing it. It is becoming increasingly difficult in our era of big data and business intelligence, where we are bombarded with an unlimited amount of available data. More than ever, digital overload defines today's workplace. More than ever, diversions are literally at our fingertips when we give in to the temptation to procrastinate, inducing what psychiatrist and attention-deficit disorders expert Edward Hallowell calls the "attention deficit trait", with characteristics echoing those of the genetically based disorder.[xxx]

As a result, here are just a handful of statistics that paint a picture of today's workforce:

- **$997 billion**: the amount of money leeched out from the U.S. economy annually, a direct correlation to findings that knowledge workers in the U.S. waste 25% of their time grappling with their huge (and growing) data streams, as reported by the Information Overload Research Group (the organization that does exist, believe it or not).[xxxi]

---

xxx   Hemp, P. (2009, September). Death By Information Overload. *Harvard Business Review.* Retrieved from https://hbr.org/2009/09/death-by-information-overload.

xxxi   Information Overload Research Group. (2011, February 03). Information Overload Research Group takes aim at data deluge in 2011. Retrieved from http://iorgforum.org/about-iorg/media-releases/.

- **-10 points**: how much our level of IQ declines when we're distracted by email and phone calls, according to a study commissioned by Hewlett-Packard.[xxxii]

- **46 times**: the average amount per day that Americans check their mobile phones, according to a 2015 study by Deloitte.[xxxiii]

- **8 billion (at least)**: the aggregate number that refers collectively to the number of times Americans check their smartphones on a daily basis (derived from average number of looks per day multiplied by the estimated 185 million smartphone users).

- **72%**: the number of organizations admitting to at least one strategic initiative failing between the years 2013–2016 due to flaws in their decision-making process, with information overload listed as one of the top contributing factors.[xxxiv]

- **80%**: the number of executives who say that flawed information has been used to make strategic decisions, with 36% adding that their organization is not coping with information overload.

Our attention spans are spiraling out of control in general; researchers at the University of California have shown that workers typically attend to a task for about three minutes before allowing themselves to be distracted by something else (usually some sort of digital communication)—and that it takes an average of 20 minutes to get back on

xxxii Hemp, P. (2009, September). Death By Information Overload. *Harvard Business Review*. Retrieved from https://hbr.org/2009/09/death-by-information-overload.

xxxiii Eadicicco, L. (2015, December 15). Americans Check Their Phones 8 Billion Times Per Day. *Time*. Retrieved from http://time.com/4147614/smartphone-usage-us-2015/.

xxxiv Senior leaders say big data, misaligned incentives and bureaucracy lead to bad decision making. (2016, February 2). *The Economic Voice*. Retrieved from https://www.economicvoice.com/senior-leaders-say-big-data-misaligned-incentives-and-bureaucracy-lead-to-bad-decision-making/.

track with the original task at hand.[xxxv] This is, after all, the era in which new dictionary terms include "FOMO" (fear of missing out), "FOBO" (fear of being offline), "nomophobia" (fear of being out of mobile phone contact), and even "email apnea" (the unconscious suspension of regular and steady breathing when people tackle their email).

Whatever the catalyst, an unlimited amount of data leads to dire and unwanted consequences. And I say *data,* because I believe "information overload" may be a misnomer. The point is to turn raw data into useful information; in collecting too much data senior executives lose the ability to parse through and filter meaningful information borne from the research, which must serve as a foundation for their strategic decision. An overreliance on data can clutter our thinking and cause us to easily lose focus on the facts which are most pressing and important for our decisions. It is the equivalent of "losing yourself in the trees" when you should be seeing the entire forest.

It leads us to *these* dire unintended consequences: "data asphyxiation", "data smog", "information fatigue syndrome", "cognitive overload", and "time famine"—a profusion of phrases coined over the past few years. Senior executives must be meticulous and picky when it comes to gathering information that is relevant to the strategic decision at hand. The need to choose the best strategic option from all available possible avenues is a daunting task in and of itself. When you layer it with the potential for unintended consequences emanating from even the best choice, it becomes obvious how critical it is for the senior executives to make the proper choice in the first place.

The trick, of course, is to learn how to control the data overload instead of letting the data overload control you. It's tricky because synthesizing information from multiple data sources demands time—something senior executives aren't notorious for having. Time must be

---

xxxv   Mark, G., Gonzalez, V., & Harris, J. (2005). No Task Left Behind? Examining the Nature of Fragmented Work (Dissertation, University of California) [Abstract]. Retrieved from http://citeseerx.ist.psu.edu/viewdoc/download?doi=10.1.1.77.7612&rep=rep1&type=pdf.

made, however: time to reflect on the implications of a decision, time to apply judgment, time to make trade-offs, time to arrive at a good strategic decision. By polluting this precious time with an overabundance of data, you only serve to increase the likelihood of missed or misinterpreted filtering.

"Lack of direction, not lack of time, is the problem. We all have twenty-four hour days."

—Zig Ziglar

The Garbage Can Model and the DIET Approach

In an article for *Administrative Science Quarterly*, Michael D. Cohen, James G. March, and Jordan P. Olsen describe the "garbage can decision-making model", the process in which executives whirl their problems and possible decisions around in a metaphorical garbage can and then people end up agreeing on whatever decision rises to the top.[xxxvi] The vast amount of data and variables produces an obvious undesirable result: executives struggle to prioritize, ensuing in the arbitrary application of data towards new choices, which leads to subpar outcomes.

Specifically, in the absence of a formal decision-making process, it seems that the authors argue that solutions arise from the haphazard interplay of four independent organization streams: problems (originating from anywhere and demanding attention), solutions (which may be created beforehand as "templates" and which can change according to preference), participants (employees, contractors, volunteers, etc.; participation is often fluid), and choice opportunities (decision-making moments brought about by demands such as deadlines or new contracts).

---

xxxvi   Cohen, M. D., March, J. G., & Olsen, J. P. (1972). A Garbage Can Model of Organizational Choice. *Administrative Science Quarterly*, 17(1), 1. doi: 10.2307/2392088.

Think of the choice opportunities as the actual "garbage cans" of the scenario; when the time comes for the garbage truck to drive through the neighborhood, organizations stuff their cans with solutions and problems, many of which are unnecessary (it's like throwing out food you don't like even though it hasn't spoiled) or irrelevant (e.g. items that belong in the recycling bin). The garbage can model seizes variables and swirls them around in a state of anarchy, based on the presumption that no organizational solution-seeking process exists.

How can we properly deal with "garbage can" decision making, then? How do we counter it? Cohen, March, and Olsen suggest that executives can begin by being much more careful with the information they choose to consider. To help filter this information, they've developed a system aptly named the "Data DIET Approach", in which DIET stands for Define, Integrate, Explore, and Test.

Define

Typically, executives tend to jump right in, leaning instinctively towards the concept of "progress" (a course of action, regardless of its ultimate relevancy) and fixating on familiar approaches they've used in the past. By fighting against this habit, you allow yourself the ability to look at a problem with a fresh perspective. Consciously opening your mind and seeking alternatives from a variety of options will reveal new questions and issues, helping to alert you to risks and potential disadvantages and therefore help to align you in the right direction as the hunt for data continues. It's a straightforward enough strategy but frighteningly underestimated by the majority of people. You needn't be one of them. Accurately define the problem and you're halfway to the solution.

Integrate

Having successfully acquired your data and morphed it into information, you must determine how to use it most effectively. Integration enables you to analyze how your options and data fit together. Visualization models can aid in this process, revealing patterns that can help you connect the dots and focus on the most effective option.

Explore

Exploration is bolstered by ties of collaboration, as emphasized in Chapter 7. Senior executives can delegate and assign distinct strategic options to different teams, having them develop a high-level outcome for each scenario. By then discussing the various collaboratively-developed results, the team can enlighten the executives as to what they forecast. Repeating this process several times while reconfiguring the teams will offer an even wider variety of potential projections. The executive must retain the obligation to make the final call, choosing to validate the direction that appears most promising once the viable options have been thoroughly presented.

Test

Test your theories every step of the way and use the process of elimination to oust whatever "solution" is irrelevant or ineffective for your scenario. Once you have a better grasp of the strategic options available, you can continue with a more disciplined data search. Test yourself to see if you have enough data by asking yourself: "how would my decision change if this data is collected?" If you already know that the information emerging from that data would not affect your decision, you don't need to waste your time (or anyone else's) delving into it.

Finally, consider the feasibility of the outcome using critical thinking and simulations. Focus on thinking strategically about your data needs and doing more with less by widening, deepening, integrating, and testing your data collection process and monitoring how it translates into valuable information. Don't let the C-suite get overwhelmed by the amount of data collected; delegate and communicate effectively without micromanaging while retaining the control and confidence that the right data has been considered. Ultimately, your goal is to ensure that executives stay focused on the big picture.

> *"There is nothing quite so useless as doing with great efficiency something that should not be done at all."*
> —Peter Drucker

Don't Get Lost in the Thick of Thin Things

It took them a while, but Keurig's executives retaliated with ways to incorporate a variety of coffees from over 70 brands. They also brought back the reusable K-cups, emphasizing that the people had spoken and that they as a corporation were listening. Instead of doubling down on its restrictive practices, the company commendably listened to customer feedback, revealing its apt leadership; good leaders must be willing to admit and learn from their mistakes. The company had regained its footing and had realigned itself with its ultimate goal. Their focus returned to the only thing which could ever really ensure corporate success: customer satisfaction.

Author Neal A. Maxwell coined the famous phrase "beware of getting lost in the thick of thin things." Apparently, he was referring to living life in general, warning people not to fall into the trap of devoting their lives to things that have little long-term value or meaning. His words are more than relevant, however, for the senior executives who are responsible for the successful implementation of their strategic decisions and struggle daily to meet great aspirations.

Indeed, it is proper implementation that will lead the company to the stated positive outcome. The outcome—not the effort—is the prize. It is the executive's responsibility to stay focused on the impending horizon and to ensure that the team's purposeful actions are aligned with it in order to deliver the future as forecasted.

Executives must fight the desire to get "into the weeds" of implementation, as it is the easiest way to risk losing sight of the end goal. Delving into the details impairs our ability to bring that high-level perspective required at times to keep the team focused on the plan. And while it is appropriate for senior leaders to stay on top of progress, it can be demotivating for employees to have a boss who insists on knowing every detail every step of the way. Don't let all your hard work backfire.

Micromanaging (as discussed in Chapter 8) and getting lost in the thick of thin things isn't just a managerial concern, either; be mindful of the level of detail your team delves into, too. Micromanagement by you or your surrogates can disempower your workforce, but it can also misguide their style as they seek to mirror your faulty approach. Whether you realize it or not, you're leading by example—remember that. Unaligned goals and teams (especially those who lose interest and ownership over the implementation of a strategy) sow the seeds for unintended consequences. Effective delegation and collaboration will help you go the distance when it comes to obtaining sufficient insight and progress.

Your primary responsibility is to keep the strategic vision on track.

"The main thing is to keep the main thing a main thing."
—Stephen R. Covey

Section III:
Something to Consider

10

The Dangerous Case of Decidophobia

"If I had to sum up in one word what makes a good manager, I'd say decisiveness. You can use the fanciest computer to gather the numbers, but—in the end—you have to set a timetable and act."

—Lee Iacocca

WATCH OUT FOR THE DRIFTERS. BEWARE THE Exegetical Thinkers. And have an eye out for those Manicheans.

They're a victimized lot, characterized by conformity and group-think tendencies, with strong symptoms of self-deception and insecurity. Side-effects include maintenance of the status quo, an infestation of "yes men", eliminated internal thought competition, and a frightening reduction of critical decision-making. Specifically, in a workplace setting, senior executives should be vigilant in deciphering the signs and containing the scattered embers of indecision before they blow up into overwhelming flames. The larger the firm, the more difficult the task, but smaller privately-held companies can be just as easily infected.

Still, there is hope.

Let's take a closer look at what we're dealing with here.

Leo Apotheker, former CEO of HP (November 2010–September 2011), starred as the tragic protagonist of one of the most infamous decisions made within the company during his tenure: the $11 billion deal for a British software company called Autonomy. Ironically, Apotheker did not seem to shoulder any autonomy for the deal, which was initiated with great ambitions and ended up simply shattering the confidence of HP's investors.

Apotheker, perhaps due to his background at multinational software corporation SAP SE, had a grand vision of moving away from PCs and tackling the software, server, and corporate tech services markets with a different PC spinoff. The problem was twofold: he never got around to deciding on a spinoff for HP's PC business and furthermore never decided whether he'd dive "all in" and brand HP as the ultimate information and software company. Autonomy was purchased with the idea that it would help position HP to execute this new strategy, but curiously it was to be run as a separate company. Talks of the PC spinoff—with several announcements regarding abrupt strategic decisions—had the market going wild with excitement . . . but nothing concrete materialized.

The idea began to tank, rousing HP's clientele's frustration and confusion. In the market's eyes, the lack of a clear, concise message came across as indecisiveness. It hurt HP's brand and slashed investor confidence. In 2011, HP's stock dropped by nearly 50% before word spread that the company would be letting Apotheker go. It was estimated that the company lost more than $30 billion in market capitalization during his brief tenure. HP Autonomy itself had already written off $8.8 billion of its value.

HP replaced Apotheker in the fall of 2011 with former eBay chief Meg Whitman. Whitman recognized exactly where HP had fallen off track and acknowledged it publicly and immediately: "The only thing we can do to regain investors' and customers' confidence is to execute," she declared once becoming CEO. "And that's what I intend to do."

Luckily for HP, it's exactly what she did.

Whitman accelerated the review of the PC business and made the decision to keep it. By April of the following year, HP had regained much of the PC market share that it had lost during what media outlets had dubbed "the period of indecision". But it remains to this day an exemplary anecdote of corporate dysfunction, the story of how "HP had lost its way".

The Study of Decidophobia

German-American philosopher and Harvard graduate Walter Kaufmann is credited with introducing us to the term "decidophobia", coining it in his 1973 book *Without Guilt and Justice: From Decidophobia to Autonomy*. His primary philosophical focus in the book was to consider how humanity simultaneously craves and dreads autonomy. By examining the inner struggle both at an individual level and a societal standpoint, Kaufmann concluded that it is natural to struggle to formulate a balance. Those who conduct fateful decisions without any apprehension for how these decisions affect others can be considered thoughtless, impulsive, or unfeeling—even menacing. Kaufmann adds that instilling fear has been a long-time method of governance to ensure social stability, while teaching the skills required for responsible decision making is a far more difficult feat (for with responsibility come obligations).

On the other hand, those who are paralyzed with the fear of wrongful outcomes to the point that they are unable to make any significant decisions are just as dangerous, as they might be too easily influenced or rendered opinionless or static. These include the people who lack the courage, confidence, or will to tackle the different sides of an argument and reach an intelligent conclusion. They would rather hand over this power to a higher authority—a parent, a government, a church—and thereby relinquish their right to speak and even think;

it may eventually get to the point that the person accepts anything argued by that authority as truth.

These are the decidophobes.

The study of decidophobia (yes, it exists!) reveals that people with this malady tend to avoid making decisions, since they harbor an immense fear of taking chances and making choices. They lack the courage to decide, worried that they'll make the wrong choice which will ensue in a dreadful outcome—and therefore decide on the easiest thing of all: to remain indecisive. The condition is generally associated with an intensely unpleasant past experience which has been branded in the individual's conscious or subconscious mind. When a perceived similar situation occurs, the decidophobe reverts to backing out.

In society decidophobia is dangerous because it is characterized by the negation of rational analysis and the need to form an unhealthy dependent relationship on someone else. Some people engage in "magical thinking", linked to the psychic world—the fallacy of attributing causal relationships that are more imagined than real. While such a mentality can be entertaining and might even be positively or negatively effective psychologically (consider the placebo effect or psychosomatic diseases), experts of anxiety relief and control theory report that people tend to turn to "magical beliefs" when feeling uncertain or insecure and lack the ability to logically respond.

Unsurprisingly, the ultimate downside of decidophobia is the loss of control over one's own life.

Like any other community, you can think of a business as a micro-society of individuals, including those of higher and lower hierarchies, who must make countless respective decisions over the course of the business's lifetime. Given that it is such an interconnected society, the outcomes of these decisions don't only affect the decider; they have the potential to impact many others within the firm. And as in any society, there will be members of the company who may not be able to handle responsibility as well and who habitually defer to "a higher authority" for direction in their professional lives as they do in their personal lives. When taken to the extreme, this condition of decision avoidance results in pushing all decisions to leadership and ultimately weighing down the executive team with an unnecessary burden.

> *"If it doesn't challenge you, it doesn't change you."*
> —Fred Devito

From Decidophobia...to Autonomy

To solve any sort of problem, remember that you must first define it. Before you tackle the implementation of a cure, you have to become aware of the condition. It is up to you, as the senior executive, to remain vigilant and ensure that your managers and employees do not become decidophobes. Dr. Walter Kaufmann helps us in this, as he has defined the following common symptoms that afflict the decidophobe. Have you noticed such recurring signals when someone in your organization attempts to make—or avoid—a decision in the workplace?

- Excessive sweating
- Muscle tension
- Dry mouth
- Dizziness or nausea
- Hyperventilation
- Feelings of emotional claustrophobia; feeling trapped or stuck
- Irrational feelings of impending disaster

Armed with this knowledge, I suggest that you perform a checkup on the various levels of management to see how critical decisions are being made. See if they are being made at the appropriate level, for instance, or if they constantly seem to be floating to a higher authority. If you diagnose an environment of decidophobia, it is essential that you investigate further to find the carrier ("patient zero") of the infection. Patient Zero might be a senior level manager who has molded a culture of fear for those below him or her, micromanaging and conditioning them to run all decisions by him or her as the higher authority. Patient Zero may just as easily be an employee or team leader who is petrified of taking on the risks and responsibilities of decision-making, regardless of how apt or capable he or she is otherwise as a professional.

Kaufmann analyzes how decidophobia can drive individuals to adopt a variety of "strategies" (Kauffman discusses ten in total) which enable them to avoid responsibility. Three such strategies which I consider most relevant and prevalent in the workplace are as follows:

The Drifters

Drifting results from a person's desire to maintain the status quo, since they realize that maintaining it means reducing the number of critical decisions that must be made. A "drifter" swims with the current, floating on the surface and letting the water carry him or her in whatever direction. According to Kaufmann, "Model A Drifters" are those who never question prevailing traditions or codes, and they abide religiously by the sacred cows of the organization. "Model B Drifters", on the other hand, reject the status quo and prefer to opt out of such establishments; they wander just as aimlessly, however, following whims instead of long-term goals. Both models believe that their lives are beyond their own control and they are characterized by a sense of despair and futility.

To uncover the Model A Drifters in your business, look within your organization for departments or areas where leaders actively work to thwart change or any initiatives designed to challenge the current environment. This typically indicates that the managers are unwilling or unable to accept the risks involved with deciding how to break free of the constraints of the status quo.

The Exegetical Thinkers

Exegetical Thinkers avoid standing up for themselves and sharing their thoughts. Their dominant fear is: *what if I'm wrong?* If others followed the Exegetical Thinker's lead—should he or she share a thought—the Exegetical Thinker would not then know what to do, since this person would be snared in a situation that calls for an evaluation of alternatives and invites the use of reason and logical assessment. In the workspace, these folks are known as "Yes Men" (or "Yes Women"). Dr. Kaufmann describes them as blind believers in the rightness of the written text or a higher authority. They tend to agree with *everything* thrown at them by their superior, believing that agreeing with authority will keep them on the boss's good side. Yes Men are unwilling to provide original ideas, opinions, or—most importantly—constructive criticism. This frees them from the risks associated with any decision, yet this tends to ruin the productivity and usefulness in the department they lead or contribute to.

Apart from hearing them literally say "yes" all the time, you can also discern them because they're usually the ones who have taken on way too much on their plates simply because they don't know how to say no. They'll agree with their boss or team on how a task will be handled, then they'll head over to another meeting with another executive who will tell them something that contradicts their original conclusion; they'll then return back to the first boss or team carrying a whole different strategy. Initially, they may appear affable, happy to help, and stress-free. A few weeks or months later, the problems brewing beneath the surface erupt: incomplete work, unmet deadlines, empty promises, and souring relationships and resentment as their peers or subordinates realize that they'll have to work twice as hard to fulfill the promises of the Yes Men.

So what's the prescription to ward off this malady? As their leader, you can take certain initiatives to train Yes Men to think for themselves. Force them to begin thinking through the decision-making process by asking them to walk through this thought process with you. Analyze how and when they change their minds. Challenge them to face difficult conversations and come to individual conclusions. Work with them and establish very clear goals for them—on a monthly, weekly, and even daily basis as much as possible. Shepherd them carefully and encourage them until they develop decision-making techniques and can intelligently delegate. It is easiest to help and train someone who exhibits motivation but lacks decision-making skills; it may be harder—even impossible—to handle someone who lacks commitment.

The Manicheans

On the surface this condition is harder to diagnosis. Manicheans are the sort of people who insist on the need for a decision, but the choice is loaded and practically seems to make itself. It's like being asked to choose between two dishes of food with the knowledge that one of them is healthy and the other is laced with poison. They classify each decision into two classifications: black vs. white, heroic vs. villainous, etc. Inconvenient facts are ignored or denied, the falsification of history becomes an indispensable crutch, and arguments that make them uncomfortable are automatically discredited. "Manichean" itself is derived from the philosophy of Manichaeism, an old religion based on *dualism*—the belief that everything can be divided neatly between good and evil.

It's a childish all-or-nothing mentality that leaves no breathing space for gray areas, for exploration and creativity and brainstorming and alternative solutions. When this type of thinking is practiced in a work setting, the symptoms appear as groupthink tendencies. This might surface when the organization strives too hard to create a culture of consensus and unanimity, rooting out independent thought and practically forcing consent. The ever-vigilant senior executive must be careful that what looks like consensus and organizational congruence is not in reality an organization infected by groupthink. Groupthink leads to blind spots and errors in decision making due to the lack of consideration for choices that oppose the prevailing beliefs.

Just What the Doctor Recommended: A Spoonful of Clarity and an Injection of Courage

Leo Apotheker's greatest mistake was his inability to make a clear decision concerning the path he desired to walk with HP, rather than spouting his indecisiveness publicly. It was not just his right as the leader to take firm executive action, but his obligation. The worst option was to float the idea that the company "might" indefinitely and vaguely spin off an extremely sizable and important portion of the business—one-third!—and never decide how to do it. This displayed the very opposite of the sort of mentality that investors and clients are attracted to and count on: confident, communicative, and intelligent management. Whether it was caution, negligence, or fear, Apotheker's hesitation to tackle the dream and morph it into a reality was exactly that which tainted and damaged his own credibility as a leader and—since it was under his indecisive command—that of the entire company itself.

Decision-making might not come easy to your organization at first, but (like pretty much anything) your people will get better with practice. It's not a necessary evil, either; it's the most straightforward and powerful way to control your firm's destiny. Specifically, it is the *only* way to control the potential unintended consequences from infecting the strategic decisions designed to produce a better future.

Don't be like Apotheker. Don't allow for the Drifters. Challenge the Exegetical Thinkers. Reject the Manicheans. Teach your organization to let go of fear and insecurity. Tell them that companies either win or they learn. Model the mentality that the only real failure is the failure to decide. Build a positive culture that believes the best course of action is to *choose*—choose progress, choose courage, and choose change when change must come. Above all, your employees should not be afraid to *choose*.

11
Creating the Future

"Without refection, we go blindly on our way, creating more unintended consequences, and failing to achieve anything useful."
—Margaret J. Wheatley

CHANCES ARE YOU'VE NOTICED THE PLETHORA OF memes floating around the internet regarding the Volkswagen emissions scandal. Go ahead and google "funny VW memes about diesel emissions" and try not to fall off your chair laughing. Some of them are ridiculously brilliant.

I'll tell you who *isn't* laughing: the Volkswagen corporation itself. They had to face multiple recalls, revocation of awards, indictments against six executives and the removal of former CEO Martin Winterkorn, criminal investigations by the Justice Department, $4.3 billion in fines, and many more billions of dollars to cover the costs of recalls. The recalls entailed more than 8.5 billion vehicles in Europe alone.

It all started in the mid-2000s, when automakers around the world confronted the biggest challenge in their industry: to create vehicles that not only met market demands for power and fuel efficiency but which would also adapt to stricter emissions regulations. Volkswagen stepped up to bat, tackling this issue creatively. Unfortunately, this creativity was not geared towards adhering to the standards; rather, the company's senior executives brainstormed how to work around them for a number of their diesel models.

They used software algorithms—which parts supplier Bosch and internal employees reportedly warned the company *not* to use in production—to cheat testers. Certain conditions usually exist in test environments which do not usually exist on the road; this software played with that weakness, as it could detect the conditions and adjust emissions accordingly. As Volkswagen would later admit, the software calibrations in three separate diesel emissions systems had a second calibration intended to run only during certification testing, therefore bypassing or defeating elements of the vehicle's emission control system.[xxxvii]

This "defeat device" worked surprisingly well for a number of years. Volkswagen even won the "Green Car of the Year Award" for the Jetta TDI in 2009 and the Audi A3 TDI. Regardless of how well the senior executives slept at night with a tainted conscience, it appeared that the company was doing splendidly. Things seemed to be going according to plan.

Until 2014, when West Virginia University researchers noticed "significantly higher in-use emissions" in a 2012 Jetta and a 2013 Passat that ran on diesel, according to the Environmental Protection Agency (EPA). This caught the attention of regulators—and, soon, the general public. Volkswagen retaliated by voluntarily recalling its diesel cars to "address emissions issues" and by explaining that the differences simply amounted to technical issues and unexpected test conditions. By July 2015, CARB and the EPA refused to certify VW's 2016 diesel lineup, making it impossible for the company to sell those cars.

xxxvii VW Diesel Crisis: Timeline of Events. (2017, April 21). Retrieved from https://www.cars.com/articles/vw-diesel-crisis-timeline-of-events-1420681251993/.

Only then did Volkswagen admit to software irregularities and cheating emissions tests. By then, the "dieselgate" scandal had caught fire, with the news swiftly circumventing the globe. Had it been a real fire, it's questionable if the smoke wouldn't have been as black as VW's diesel emissions.

"Consequences are unpitying."
—George Eliot

Five Qualities of Effective Strategists and Performers

A study was conducted among nearly 700 executives across a variety of industries, based on a survey that asked respondents to rate the effectiveness of the top leaders within their firm. The researchers sought to illuminate the difference between stumbling companies (shown to be those that compete on the basis of economies of scale, lucrative assets, or diversification) and sustainably successful companies (capabilities-driven organizations that owe their success to distinctively providing three things: value, a powerhouse of capabilities, and coherence between their strategy and capabilities).[xxxviii] In their quest to determine how many leaders excelled at strategy and execution, the researchers revealed some sobering results: a meager 16% of top leaders were rated very effective at either strategy or execution. Only 8% were rated as very effective at both. On a heartening note, the research did suggest that those who become better strategists exhibit a higher probability of improving their skills of execution as well; this, too, is a scenario of interrelated best practices.

---

xxxviii Mainardi, C. P., & Leinwand, P. (2013, October 28). What drives a company's success? Highlights of survey findings. Retrieved from http://www.strategyand.pwc.com/reports/what-drives-a-companys-success.

Top Leaders' Effectiveness at Strategy Execution and Development
Few are good at both.

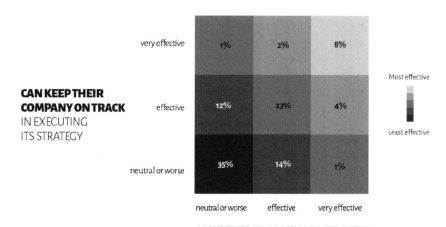

SOURCE "WHAT DRIVES A COMPANY'S SUCCESS?" BY PAUL LEINWAND AND CESARE MAINARDI, 2013   © HBR.ORG

The same researchers concluded that there are five distinct leadership qualities that, when cultivated, allow senior executives to enhance their abilities to both set strategies and encourage execution of the decision within the organization. By understanding and mastering these qualities, you can gain the ability to lower the incidence of unintended consequences, creating a stable company culture while also enjoying a more predictable future.

- **Commit to an identity as a leader.** You are the symbolic figurehead of your company in the sense that you are the primary role model. Committing to leadership means living up to your greatest potential to the best of your ability, for you are selling a message about your identity as the core of a brand. Demonstrating the courage of your corporate convictions—your values, your mission, your goals—you are the person who defines and develops the influence and impact needed to rouse your people and build your empire.

- **Translate strategy into everyday actions.** It's a balancing act to get your hands dirty but to not get too far lost in the details, as we've emphasized in prior chapters. You're the only one who has the full picture at hand; only you can simultaneously access the short-term and long-term vision of your organization. By fusing the ability to avoid micro-management (as Martha Stewart learned the hard way) and the art of controlling a situation (as realized too late by Volkswagen's executives), you can ensure congruence during the phases of strategy and execution while retaining your focus on the long-term vision as well.

- **Put your culture to work for you.** As the leader, you are the gardener of your corporate culture; whatever you culti-vate will be sure to bloom. If you value and practice life-long learning, collaboration, ethical behavior, and transparency, you will build a cooperative and ethical learning organiza-tion around you. If you plant the seeds of accountability and authenticity, that is what you will find before you. If you act like you emerged from a remote corner office, that is how you will be treated. Always remember that you are an integral part of your corporate environment; by instilling elements of trust, ownership, and aligned goals, you have the power to harness and leverage individual and team efforts for the collective good of the company.

- **Prioritize your time wisely.** You will always be busy, I promise you. Work never ends; we do, however. We burn out, we get sick, we get exhausted, we die (sobering, but true). The time we are given meanwhile may not be a lot—if used wisely, however, it may be enough. If you constantly find yourself stressed out, in panic mode, or way behind schedule, you're doing it wrong. As a leader, you must prioritize your personal resources very carefully—including, above all, your time and your attention. What is urgent and what is important? What are high- and low-level activities? Avoid squandering your time on ever-present immediate demands at the expense of strategic decisions that only the C-suite is qualified to make. If you focus on what's important and strategize proactively, you will always have time.

- **Shape the future**—or it'll shape you. Given the ability to strategize for the long term and to see the entire picture, you are the one with the capability to define—and then direct—the direction in which you'd like your business to go. You must therefore be keenly aware of the constant challenges arising within and beyond your business, and (equally imperative) realize that the change must begin within yourself. Through self-awareness and accountability, you can build a loyal management team whose members are also willing to admit when they need to grow, change, and learn from mistakes; such characteristics of humility and the drive for excellence can then be echoed throughout all the levels of the company. This in turn enables you to create and implement—on all levels—a robust development plan to align and guide your organization forward.

"Sometimes when I consider what tremendous consequences come from little things, I am tempted to think there are no little things."

—Bruce Barton

The Road to "Dieselgate" … and the Alternative

There's plenty of blame to go around regarding the Volkswagen scandal.

The company—knowing that top management would face additional lawsuits and fines if convicted—tried claiming that its executives knew nothing of the illegal software, blaming instead "a few rogue engineers". The company did admit that its managerial board did comprehend the existence and use of their illegal defeat device a month prior to the EPA's Notice of Violation issue, but they were under the impression that defeat devices didn't incur significant punishments.[xxxix]

Whether or not this is the case, Volkswagen's wrongdoing (and blame-shifting) is a glaring example of how the "blind eye"—purposeful or neglectful—of senior executives can contribute to enormous unintended consequences. Even if the VW engineers were to blame (and at least three were suspended over the emissions issue), it is their senior managers who are at greater fault for failing at the basic "management" aspect of their managerial and leadership positions.

Returning to the original theory of Dr. Merton as expressed in the beginning of this book, I am a staunch believer that every purposeful human action has the potential for at least one unintended or unanticipated outcome. My goal has been to guide you through the business battlefield and point out some of the endless examples showing the catalysts and concerns of unintended consequences. If we are willing to learn from the experiences of other business executives, we do not need to repeat the same mistakes over and over.

Merton's research provided the context from which to begin our study of the role of unintended consequences in a business setting, and to focus specifically on how they can negatively impact you, as a senior leader, as well as the performance of your business. The real-world stories throughout the prior chapters have illustrated how unintended consequences can indeed emerge from the fertile ground of Merton's five primary causes.

---

xxxix   Geuss, M. (2016, March 03). Volkswagen details what top management knew leading up to emissions revelations. Retrieved from https://arstechnica.com/cars/2016/03/volkswagen-says-ceo-was-in-fact-briefed-about-emissions-issues-in-2014/.

1. Ignorance

2. Error

3. Immediate Interests

4. Basic Values

5. Self-Defeating Prophecies

Knowing the causes without a prescription to cure them, however, would not be a satisfactory outcome. We did, therefore, also examine six best practices that form the protocol designed to vaccinate your company against an infestation of unintended consequences. These practices are all interrelated, since working on one can help incite the practice of the others; by working on each of them, you accelerate the positive protecting qualities of them all.

1. Slow down

2. Learn

3. Clarify

4. Delegate and collaborate

5. Conscious control

6. Focus

We cannot completely foresee the future. I stand by my original statement that crystal balls don't exist to help us to avoid unintended consequences. We can, however, work to define and create the future to the best of our ability. The more resources and wisdom at our disposal, the more accurate and effective our efforts will be.

I've personally been fascinated by the effects of unintended consequences in business for nearly a decade. Each year, I discover new examples of how companies are ravaged by them; each year, I see executives who instill best practices and purge themselves from the plague of unexpected and negative outcomes.

Through my work and through countless sessions of peer learning and peer mentoring, I have discovered that each senior executive has constructed a decision ecosystem designed to enable better strategic business decisions. I have also found that the more robust an ecosystem, the more likely it is for that executive to successfully anticipate and counter future unintended consequences. Such an ecosystem can serve as a powerful barrier to inoculate your business from the "rats" of your industry. By cultivating a powerful decision-making process with the steps outlined in this book, and by adding a healthy dose of peer learning from executives who are outside your firm, you will strengthen your ecosystem and improve your company's performance.

The anecdotes in this book are in no way exhaustive. I'm always interested in learning more. If you have a story or have a direct experience with a case of unintended consequences and would like to share it with me, please feel free to contact me at RFranzi@criticalmassforbusiness.com and I encourage you to also visit my website at www.criticalmassforbusiness.com.

"Wisdom consists of the anticipation of consequences."
—Norman Cousins

12
The Pervasiveness of Unintended Consequences

"It is … highly probable that from the very beginning, apart from death, the only ironclad rule of human experience has been the Law of Unintended Consequences."
—Ian Tattersall

A World of Invisible Hands and Powerful Butterflies…

In 1776, Adam Smith coined **"the invisible hand"** in his book *The Wealth of Nations*. He defined it more precisely in Book IV, Chapter II, as when "[an individual], by directing that industry in such a manner as its produce may be of the greatest value, he intends only his own gain, and he is in this, as in many other cases, led by an invisible hand to promote an end which was no part of his intention. Nor is it always the worse for the society that it was not part of it." In other words: an individual acts entirely in his or her own interests and this behavior provokes unintended consequences, either positive or negative, to his or her surroundings.

"The invisible hand" is a concept that resides in the heart of the capitalist model and the free market economic theory, and the term maintains as much relevance and fame as the book itself does to this day. It stems from the free market participants' inherent and individual inclination to enhance their own wellbeing. Driven by their own needs, they compete and progress and succeed, involuntarily (but not unwillingly) benefitting society at large. This is applicable to human behavior beyond theories of markets and economies, of course. Comparative advantage, thinking at the margin, and the benefits of trade can all be traced back to this cornerstone concept; entire books and university departments have dedicated themselves to examining the intricacies of "the invisible hand".

In the business sphere, good leadership means respecting, understanding, and harnessing the power of "the invisible hand". Failures embodied in negative unintended consequences in business can often be traced back to well-educated (and often well-meaning) executives trying to modify market behavior to their advantage without considering all the potential consequences on a grander scale. Ironically, these same executives many times bemoan government attempts at market regulation, not realizing that they are mirroring the same mentality and could easily fail in a similar fashion. Relatively free markets without a central authoritative planner have proven to be more optimal for effective resource allocation. Attempts to withhold an individual's ability to exercise discretion in pursuing his or her interests haven't been the most successful historically (they are the fodder for resentful, repressed, and eventually rebellious societies—no characteristic of which is ideal for a healthy and progressive economy or any national ecosystem).

Nearly two centuries later, in 1972, American mathematician and MIT meteorology professor Edward Lorenz coined **"the butterfly effect"**, basing it on his research regarding how small actions in one place can lead to exponentially larger events. While working on a computer program that simulated weather patterns, Lorenz repeated a simulation and rounded off one of the 12 variables (a tiny alteration from .506127 to .506). He discovered that *this* drastically transformed the program's entire pattern.

Lorenz's speech at the American Association for the Advancement of Science was in fact entitled: "Predictability: Does the Flap of a Butterfly's Wings in Brazil Set a Tornado in Texas?" He was originally referring to how behavior in the atmosphere is unstable regarding perturbations of small amplitude. After condensing his findings into a paper titled "Deterministic Nonperiodic Flow", Lorenz's conclusion was adopted as one of the cornerstone principles of the Chaos Theory in mathematics, challenging society's beliefs of a "clockwork universe" and offering deeper insight (that small changes can have large consequences), along with a weighty repercussion: it's practically impossible to absolutely forecast the future.

In our context, the frail butterfly perfectly embodies the innocuous nature of decisions that can appear small but can, in fact, have overwhelming consequences—aptly illustrated by the tornado metaphor, as it is an inarguably overwhelming phenomenon of nature. Lorenz's "butterfly effect" theory provides some scientific context for us to understand why unintended consequences are so prevalent, and this concept—that small changes in the input can have drastic changes in the output—holds true beyond the "hard sciences". Each day, when dealing with more fluid or subjective topics like building a brand image or cultivating a corporate culture, you'll be faced with "fine lines" that can undergo "tiny alterations" that can transform a company as drastically as Kafka's human-to-cockroach metamorphosis.

Good leadership is shown through prudence in understanding which inputs matter and how. The "butterfly effect" is also helpful in conceptualizing the idea that doing the right things can be significantly more important than doing many things; in brief, quality over quantity. Leaders must identify the inputs that can lead to exponentially larger outputs and align their teams to maximize their efficiency, whether this is through a technological innovation or by boosting employee morale through non-traditional means.

And what about dueling with the invisible hand?

Instead of trying to make decisions for the market, strive to *be* the best decision in your market. Incentivize individuals to gravitate towards your product or service—whether to work for it or to buy of it—and you will reap the benefits of the invisible hand's power. You do this by focusing on real-world value, not on short-term gimmicks or promotions meant to hit arbitrary metrics. In the day-to-day grindstone, it can be easier to revert to tunnel vision and look for short-term "growth hacks" such as fees or temporary behavior modifiers.

Adding value is the only thing that allows good leaders to keep their organizations thriving. It's cliché only because it's true. No organization is likely capable of—nor would benefit from—changing the law that Adam Smith defined in 1776. Instead of attempting to force a change of human nature, successful leaders instead acknowledge the invisible hand and focus on enticing people to *want* to gravitate towards their organizations because of the real value provided.

Who Moved My Cheese? (And Can They Get Me a Different Type Instead?)

Starbucks: a widely successful conglomerate in the coffee industry and the best friend of countless coffeeholics around the world. If you haven't drunk from it, it's practically impossible that you haven't heard *of* it. As immense and popular as this brand has been and inarguably continues to be, it hasn't been without its own episodes of unintended consequences. One of the most memorable has got to be its introduction of stinky breakfast sandwiches back in 2007.

Howard Schultz, Starbucks' CEO, presented the case in a *Newsweek* article a few years later in 2011: "For me, the most symbolic representation of how Starbucks in 2007 was losing its magic was the warm breakfast sandwich. I'd resisted the idea of serving sandwiches in our stores from the start, though I understood why they made financial sense. Our warm sandwiches gained a loyal following and drove up sales and profits. The more popular they became, the more our baristas had to heat them in warming ovens. And when they did, the sandwiches would inevitably drip and sizzle in the ovens, releasing a pungent smell. The rich, hearty coffee aroma in the stores was overwhelmed by singed Monterey Jack, mozzarella, and, most offensively, cheddar. Where was the magic in burnt cheese?"[xl]

Where indeed?

Schultz's insightful hindsight is right on the money: while Starbucks' insertion of the breakfast sandwiches to expand their product offering in order to complement their premium line beverage and raise their instore revenues *did* result in initial success (i.e. an increase in instore sales), it had a dangerous and unexpected repercussion that Starbucks luckily caught whiff of—literally—in the nick of time.

Starbucks executives hadn't thought things all the way through, otherwise they may have realized that the smell of the sandwiches— English Muffins, bacon, and very strong-smelling cheese—would certainly overpower the delicate and delicious coffee aroma that had always been synonymous with the prestigious Starbucks experience. Starbucks was gaining revenue, yet this came at the expense of losing the luster that made it an industry leader.

Fortunately for the company, CEO Schultz was able to acknowledge and address the problem quickly and effectively. Making an important strategic decision, he pulled the stinky sandwiches in early 2008, confirming that maintaining the store's atmosphere (staying true to the brand) was more important than short-term profits. It was a courageous move, but necessary; it can be hard to walk away from a product that is profitable, but failing to do so—if that product hurts your overall brand and business objectives—can produce far more negative results in the long-term and even result in the organization's downfall (think Samsung's Note 7 explosions and Red Lobster's downsizing fiasco).

---

xl   Schultz, H. (2011, March 13). *Newsweek*. Retrieved from http://www.newsweek.com/saga-stinky-cheese-66167.

By staying true to its brand image and focusing on what differentiated it from the market, Starbucks circumnavigated this situation successfully and admirably. Learning from their mistakes, they did additional research and testing to determine how they could "do sandwiches right". In June 2008, they released a revamped breakfast sandwich selection using techniques (moving the cheese to the top of the sandwich, lowering the baking temperature, etc.) and ingredients (better qualities with milder smells) that didn't conflict with the store aroma or vibe. "The result was a breakfast offering that was worthy of our coffee," Howard Schultz attests.

And that's how the brand got its mojo back.

Grab a Bag, Game the System: The Freebie-Lover's Guide to Flying

In the ever-competitive airline industry, maximizing efficiency is a major concern. In an effort to gain a competitive advantage and boost margins in any way practical, many big players in the airline industry began implementing checked luggage fees in 2008. They probably believed that it was a wise decision despite the likelihood for some amount of customer backlash (because, let's face it, increased prices— fees or taxes—don't make any customer giddy with joy). Unfortunately for the airlines that implemented this new fee, they overlooked a critical flaw: carry-on bags were exempt from the fees.

Oh, there's more. Best of all? Bringing a carry-on that was just *slightly* too big for the overhead bin resulted in a *free* checked bag.

So guess what that meant?

A 2010 Consumer Reports survey ranked baggage fees as airline passengers' #1 irritation—ranked even higher than pet peeves such as crying children. And yet baggage fees have proliferated, allowing airlines to charge different customers different prices (like a "pay as you go" cellphone plan that lets customers "self-sort"), along with

127

a second rationale of changing passenger behavior (to travel with carry-on luggage only) in order to lower airline operating costs.[xli] With this loophole of bringing a carry-on that was just slightly too big and getting it checked for free, passengers were enthusiastic to realize that they got their bags freely checked *and* would have said bags returned to them at the arrival gate (which spared them the inconvenience of going to baggage claim).

People respond to incentives; it's human nature. By charging a fee for checked bags but allowing carry-ons to board flights for free, the airlines created a clear incentive for customers to squeeze everything they possibly could into as large a carry-on as they could reasonably haul along with them. People are generally loss-averse, plus they don't think about how one could escalate into a logistical nightmare if everyone else does the same incident (e.g. one individual with a slightly oversized carry-on isn't a big deal ... unless *everyone does it*).

Airlines *did* want to shape customer behavior, but they didn't weigh in the unintended consequences of flyers learning to "game the system", perverse incentivizing, and the downside of logistics issues. Huge messes were created with gate personnel and flight attendants tagging, storing, and retrieving long lines of luggage at the gate, causing passenger frustration and overall lowering both customer satisfaction and airline employee morale.

Always consider what you're incentivizing.

Why Didn't You Call? (You're Stuck in a Hotel with Dial-Up Internet? Oh ...)

"Welcome to your hotel, we hope you enjoy your stay!" is the desire and mission statement of every single hotel across the nation. Hotels discovered a new challenge to attaining this goal in the 1990s during

xli   Anderson, T. (2015, August 03). Who Benefits from Airline Baggage Fees? Retrieved from https://insight.kellogg.northwestern.edu/article/who-benefits-from-airline-baggage-fees.

the early days of dial-up modem access to the internet, when they were getting severely weighed down by the use of their telephone switches and systems. To fight back, they decided to institute a connection fee for using the phone for dial-up access. The logic behind this decision was that the fees would dissuade people from using the telephone lines for dial-up, allowing other hotel customers to make their regular phone calls more frequently and easily.

On the surface, it isn't an unreasonable premise. Fees are a common way to deter undesirable behavior. The fatal flaw, however, manifested in the fact that the fee was *connection based*. From a consumer perspective, this meant that it was cheaper to hold on to a connection for an extended period—say, all day—rather than to just use the connection as needed. If you rented a room and wanted to check your email when you woke up and before bed, you had the option to disconnect when you were done in the morning (freeing the line for other hotel visitors) and connect later again (thus paying two connection fees) ... *or* to connect once in the morning (leaving the line tied up and unavailable for anyone else all day) and check again before going to bed (thus paying only one fee). Viewing the options from the consumer's perspective, it's obvious to see why this plan backfired. Hotels practically provided the incentive to keep the phone lines busy when they weren't needed.

So again, yes, hotel executives did manage to modify customer behavior—and, again, that modification took on an unintended direction that simply exacerbated the problem that they'd been trying to solve. You could certainly argue that hotel executives didn't do their due diligence in considering how their clients would respond to the fees; they did not fully explore the problem they were trying to resolve. It may have made more sense to charge for access that was based on the amount of bandwidth consumed (charge a fee for actual usage), invest in increased telephone line infrastructure, or even look for a simple marketing technique to modify behavior.

In each scenario, the executives would still have to consider: *how would our individual guests respond?*

Good leaders master the ability to examine the full picture, learning to consider all aspects of a business decision in order to understand how their target audience will respond. They must look beneath the surface (fees discourage use, so—supposedly—problem solved) and drill down to the realities of consumer, employee, and market behavior. Thinking this scenario through may have caused them to realize that while fees on connections *will* minimize discrete connection attempts, they will *also* increase the duration of each connection and provide a disincentive to release the phone line once the connection has been established.

The Best Argument You Can Make for Not Cleaning Your Room: A Bacteriologist's Medical Breakthrough

You may know of a positive (serendipitous) unintended consequence now known as **Penicillin**—and you may have also heard how a certain bacteriologist—Dr. Alexander Fleming—stumbled upon its discovery. In September of 1928 at St. Mary's Hospital in London, Dr. Fleming returned to his lab to find that some mold had developed in some of his Petri dishes left unattended. He examined the dishes and discovered that the mold—called *Penicillium Notatum*—seemed to prevent the growth of the bacteria staphylococci (which can cause a multitude of diseases).

The scope of this unintended benefit? *Massive.* As the bacteriologist famously wrote about that day: "When I woke up on September 28th, 1928, I certainly didn't plan to revolutionize all medicine by discovering the world's first antibiotic, or bacterial killer, but I guess that was exactly what I did."

Over the weeks that followed, Dr. Fleming did his due diligence in vetting the seemingly groundbreaking discovery by testing to confirm that the mold not only stunted the growth of staphylococci, but that it could also indeed be leveraged to fight infections. Dr. Fleming himself did not have the resources or background to refine the mold into a useable product; his work was built upon by Dr. Howard Florey, the director of the Sir William Dunn School of Pathology at Oxford University. Dr. Florey's team, including biochemist Dr. Ernst Chain, worked arduously to create a viable treatment based on Dr. Fleming's findings. In 1941, in conjunction with American scientists in Illinois, they worked to develop a means of mass production for penicillin. The drug received a "trial by fire" during WWII, ensuing in demonstrative numbers; the death rate from bacterial pneumonia was at 18% during WWI, whereas it dropped to less than 1% during WWII thanks to this new wonder treatment.

The road to success—beginning from this initial discovery in London in 1928 to the first successful treatment of a civilian with penicillin in 1942 at New Haven Hospital in Connecticut—was constructed with hard work and made possible by teamwork. While the story of Dr. Fleming's accidental discovery of penicillin has become well-known over the years, it is less known that this was not one serendipitous event that occurred in a vacuum and changed the world overnight. On the contrary, it was the result of a number of dedicated professionals working together to leverage one key discovery to make a real medical breakthrough.

Penicillin was basically the unintended consequence of a bacteriologist not keeping his workplace particularly tidy. If I'd known that at a much younger age, my parents would have had *quite* the struggle in getting me to clean my room.

McDonald's McPicks: Who's Actually Lovin' It?

McDonald's might really love to believe that everyone's singing **"I'm lovin' it"** as they make a purchase. And sometimes, some people might be. Regarding the McPick 2 Deal and all-day breakfast offers initiated throughout 2015–2016, I'm pretty sure the fast-food chain's employees and franchise partners were singing a rather different tune beneath their breath.

This promotion—allowing customers to choose two items for $5, and offering select breakfast items during lunch and dinner—was launched with the primary goal of increasing guest traffic. Initially, you can argue that McDonald's succeeded in this goal. They drove up their sales growth after a two-year decline…until the results appeared as short-lived as the customers' enthusiasm. McDonald's sale-store sales grew 5.4% in the first quarter of the year, then dropped to only 1.5%.

And while afternoon and evening sales increased, McDonald's overall revenue simultaneously fell 3.6%.

By most accounts, the promotion strongly contributed to the day-part sales growth and can, in those terms, be qualified as successful. The promotions were not without their unintended consequences, however. Surveyed franchisees complained that this company strategy had cut into profit margins and furthermore led to customer exploitation: customers found an incentive to trade down to cheaper breakfast items later in the day. Some franchisees had predicted this, calling the all-day breakfast "gimmicky" and "a Band-Aid to help us get through the next couple of quarters."[xlii]

Had the McDonald's executives listened to their business partners, they may have been able to implement a different sort of plan. It's a bad sign if those closest to the customer base object to a plan, for their perspectives often have more merit than executives account for. Good leadership means keeping an ear to the ground and listening to the rumbles of the market in order to understand how customers and employees respond to ideas and decisions. McDonald's fell into the

---

xlii   Peterson, H. (2016, July 27). McDonald's franchisees had an ominous prediction—and now it's coming true. *Business Insider.* Retrieved from http://www.businessinsider.com/mcdonalds-posts-second-quarter-results-2016-7.

trap of trading profit for volume, knowing that volume *is* an important driver for growth but mistaking short-term metrics for sustainable growth.

Pfizer: "Sure, We Meant to Do That."

Dr. Merton identified times when unintended consequences are actually *pleasant* unintended consequences and called this serendipity or luck. They are unintended, but turn out to be neither unwelcome nor unpleasant.

Pharmaceutical giant Pfizer experienced one such happy accident. In the 1990s, this company had made significant investments in attempting to develop a treatment for heart disease conditions including high blood pressure and angina. One of the drugs developed during this period was Sildenafil—or, as it's more commonly known, **Viagra**. Phase one of the clinical trials indicated that the drug wasn't great at achieving the purpose it was designed for, but it did have a fascinating, unintended side effect: eliminating erectile dysfunction.

Now fondly referred to as the "little blue pill", Viagra has since transformed into a very profitable pharmaceutical product, taking the market by storm in 1998. From 2003–2016, Viagra generated an insane amount of over $1.5 billion in annual revenue, peaking at $2.05 billion in 2012.

Consistent with its origins as an unintended consequence, Viagra has been reportedly used for a variety of purposes that delineate even from its consequential purpose of encouraging erections. There have been reports of the drug being used by pilots to stay alert, by young males as a performance-enhancing recreational drug, and even as a treatment for some retinal disorders.

This case study confirms Dr. Merton's research that unintended consequences are neither inherently good nor bad. Sometimes, they can unfurl to reveal unintended benefits or new opportunities arising from our purposeful actions. Of course, it is still up to us to analyze and harness such consequences to our greatest advantage, however possible; success is grounded strongly on the observation and review of the results of a business decision or project that then enables us to identify new growth opportunities. While the pharmaceutical industry is, by its very nature, more focused on "side effects" than many other sectors, good leaders regardless of industry should consider this as an exemplary mentality.

Pfizer scored with one of the most popular pharmaceutical drugs of the last two decades not because they started out with a plan to create it, but because they paid attention to the side effects (literally) and acted upon their opportunities. Whatever the scenario—pharmaceutical giants having an "aha" moment during clinical trials, tech startups releasing a minimum viable product and tweaking it based on market feedback, or manufacturers improving a product line based on quality analysis—gathering feedback, adjusting accordingly, and fostering the ability to frame "failures" as learning opportunities will make a world of difference.

This pharmaceutical giant has had its sampling of negative unintended consequences, too. Pfizer produced a drug called **Chantix** in 2006; on the surface, this prescription medicine was supposedly aligned with a noble goal: to help people stop smoking. Unfortunately, it was also paired with a number of extremely unfavorable and unintended consequences (a.k.a. "common side-effects"). As of 2016 on the RxList, these include: months-long nausea, stomach pain, indigestion, constipation, flatulence, vomiting, headaches, tiredness, unusual dreams, insomnia, and a dry or foul-tasting mouth.[xliii]

Just a bit worrisome, no?

In 2009, Pfizer was required by the FDA to add a black box warning (the most severe warning label available) on their product. They were

xliii   Ogbru, O. (2016). Common Side Effects of Chantix (Varencline) Drug Center (M. Stoppler, Ed.). Retrieved from http://www.rxlist.com/chantix-side-effects-drug-center.htm

later sued by patients who allegedly experienced suicidal thoughts and other psychiatric disturbances while taking Chantix. In 2013, Pfizer settled such litigations with over 2,700 state and federal lawsuits, took a $272 million charge to cover the costs, and allocated another $15 million to address the remaining claims; none of this, of course, was included in Pfizer's goal statement when they launched the drug. Unintended consequences snowballed to create more unintended consequences leading to significant unplanned costs and a tarnished reputation.

In 2014, Pfizer requested for the FDA to remove their black-box warning label, complaining that it hurt their sales; they stressed that the benefit of quitting smoking outweighed the potential (but severe) side-effects of the drug, furthermore stating that the evidence of causality wasn't clear enough to warrant a black-box label. The FDA ruled to leave the warning on the box, later determining that Chantix may increase heart-attack risks along with mental disturbances, while agreeing that smoking poses its own array of risks. The latest revisions to Chantix's black-box label include the treatment's potential unintended consequences of seizures, angioedema and hypersensitivity, self-harmful behavior and increased hostility, and skin rashes with mucosal lesions.[xliv]

In a nutshell: an ounce of prevention is worth a pound of cure—both when it comes to strategizing for corporate decisions *and* when taking the time to consider if you should start smoking. Don't overcomplicate life. Think proactively.

Something You'll Love More Than You Were Supposed To: Vodafone India's Adorable ZooZoos

Do you know of the **ZooZoos**? If you don't, you're in for a treat: check

---

xliv   *Your Quit Plan*. Plan to Quit Cards]. (2016, October). Pfizer Inc. Retrieved from http://www.chantix.com/sites/default/themes/bootstrap_chantix/pdf/pp_chm_usa_1297_plan_to_quit_cards.pdf.

them out on YouTube. If you *do* know of them, you're most likely in love with them ... just like a huge population of Vodafone users in India.

The ZooZoos—adorable white creatures with ballooned bodies and expressive egg heads—were the brainchild of Ogilvy & Mather, an NY-based agency hired by Vodafone to create ads that would help the multinational telecommunications company rebrand itself in a way that would promote its value-added services. It was a very significant potential margin opportunity for Vodafone India, and the agency apparently did its homework well. The 30 new Vodafone ads—produced within 10 days and shot in Cape Town, South Africa—were an instant hit. When Vodafone launched the ZooZoos on Twitter in April 2016, it generated an estimated 90 million impressions in *two days*. At the time of this book's creation, it still reigns as Vodafone's most-loved brand mascot.

An interesting unintended consequence in this scenario was the degree to which the character became so immensely popular. ZooZoo posters and other paraphernalia flooded the market. The executives judged that the advertising campaign had been a huge success—until Ogilvy & Mather admitted that the fictional characters had become even more popular than the service they'd sought to advertise, practically stealing the brand's marketing thunder for the margin-rich, value-added services.

The focus got shifted from what was advertised to who was advertising it. The anticipated growth in number of value-added services didn't occur. As a result, the character was taken off the air ... which in turn disappointed customers, something else Vodafone didn't see coming. So, yes, the much-loved pale little ZooZoo was brought back.

Can You Take the Heat? (Because You're About to be Canned)

Ah, the Miami Heat. This American professional basketball team is based (spoiler alert) in Miami, and compete in the NBA as a member of the league's Eastern Conference Southeast Division. They've been committed to building a team that could consistently compete for and win NBA championships. To their great delight, they landed superstar LeBron James in 2010—they also gained Chris Bosh and re-signed Dwayne Wade.

It was looking like a *spectacular* year for the Miami Heat. In fact, they were experiencing such a rush in orders for season tickets leading up to the official announcement of the Big 3, they decided to stop ticket sales on July 8th, just hours before LeBron James famously announced he would join the team; the Miami Heat sales team started a waiting list for season tickets with thousands of names on it. People were unbelievably excited to seize an opportunity to watch basketball history in the making.

One group that was forced to trade excitement for disappointment—and who didn't see that disappointment coming—were 30 employees who were told they were losing their jobs on July 10th. With the season ticket inventory "exhausted", the company claimed in a report broadcasted by *Sun Sentinel*, "we no longer require a season ticket sales team to sell tickets," adding that the size of the sales staff depended solely on the supply and demand of the season ticket inventory.[xlv]

Reportedly the employees made a base salary and commission, with some of them offered extended benefits and severance of even a year's salary. However, this isn't the first time the Heat has unexpectedly and suddenly pushed employees out of the picture. In 2003, they'd surprised their entire staff with 10% pay cuts after back-to-back losing seasons, and fired about 20 employees due to a faltering economy in May 2009.

---

xlv   Talalay, S. (2010, July 30). With season tickets sold out, Heat fires season sales staff. Retrieved from http://articles.sun-sentinel.com/2010-07-30/sports/sfl-heat-season-ticket-staff-fired-20100730_1_individual-game-tickets-staff-writer-ira-winderman-sales.

As you can guess for yourself, this doesn't do wonders for Miami Heat's **staff engagement** (much less its turnover rate). And in case you're wondering how much *that* matters, just take a glance at the following statistics, amassed by Dale Carnegie Training and MSW:

- $11 billion is lost annually due to employee turnover.
- Engaged employees are characterized by: enthusiasm, inspiration, empowerment, and confidence.
- Companies with engaged employees outperform those without by up to 202%.
- 71% of all employees are not fully engaged; only 29% are.
- 80% of employees who are dissatisfied with their direct manager are disengaged.
- 70% of employees who lack confidence in the abilities of senior leadership are not fully engaged.[xlvi]

I'm not aware of the current employee morale and culture within the Heat's organization today, but my educated guess is that it's one of great trepidation. It is not generally wise to breed insecurity within your company; an unstable and fearful team is far less likely to be happy, loyal, or motivated to your corporate cause and mission. Many leaders struggle to understand why they can't operate more efficiently and turn to drastic solutions in order to see immediate results. Instead, they should realize that there is in fact significant utility in learning what would make their existing team members happy and more motivated (and a mass layoff of their coworkers doesn't usually have that effect). The Heat may have been in a unique position where they felt the tradeoff between business employee morale and cutting costs was worth it, but a plethora of studies have indicated the tangible benefits to keeping employees engaged and

xlvi   The Importance of Employee Engagement [Infographic]. (n.d.). Retrieved from http://www.dalecarnegie.com/employee-engagement/engaged-employees-infographic/.

happy—even if it doesn't seem to have obvious "savings" in the short term.

That's called a long-term investment.

The Curious Cases of Barbara Streisand and Thomas Midgley

Unintended consequences may be tracked back to the actions of an entire organization—and usually to the firm's C-suite who made the final decision—but can just as easily be triggered by the actions of a sole person (either representing themselves or an organization). One case in point is American singer, songwriter, actress, and director Barbara Streisand, who has become one of the most successful personalities in show biz, and who has been credited for inspiring the term **"the Streisand Effect"**.

It began in 2003, when the California Coastal Records Project—an innocuous organization that's supposed to maintain photographs of much of California's coastline as possible—unintentionally included Barbara Streisand's home in one of their pictures. They'd merely been recording photos of the coast for their records; just doing their job. Unfortunately, Ms. Streisand considered this photograph a violation of her privacy.

She filed a lawsuit against photographer Kenneth Adelman, seeking $50 million in damages to protect her privacy by making the California Coastal Records Project take the picture offline so that it wouldn't be visible to the public. Ironically, due to the publicity surrounding the lawsuit, many more people heard of the picture's existence and looked it up on the internet (as you may be doing right now...). The photographing had been benign, and not an attempt to invade anyone's privacy. There had been little interest in the picture prior to the lawsuit filing—it'd been seen a grand total of *six times*, two of those times by Streisand's lawyers—so the lawsuit actually served as a great way to market the picture (racking up over a million views). Streisand lost the case and was forced to pay over $155,000 in the photographer's legal fees. The lawsuit also resulted in negative publicity for Streisand, as it was seen as frivolous and flying in the face of free speech.

Not quite what she'd intended.

The associated press used the photograph multiple times, leveraging on the buzz surrounding the lawsuit; the "Streisand Effect" is now associated with the unintended outcomes related to frivolous lawsuits. It's a textbook example of the timeless warning to "choose your battles". Streisand's best strategy would have been to ignore the picture altogether, even in the interest of maintaining privacy; without the significant star power associated with her name and the juicy media story squeezed from the lawsuit, interest in the photograph probably would have remained very trivial. And while there is an argument to be made for standing up for one's beliefs, it doesn't seem that there was a legitimate privacy concern worth fighting for here—and certainly not one worth $50 million.

While my focus is on the prudent and well-rounded business decisions of good leadership, there is this aspect to consider too, regardless of which side of the Streisand Effect you find yourself on: on the flip side, there's a (short-term) marketing benefit for smaller organizations or firms that can get the attention of a bigger fish in the public eye. Streisand's fiasco and her share of unintended consequences translated into unintended benefits for Adelman: money, righteousness, *and* publicity.

Because now you know about the California Coastal Records Project, yes?

Thomas Midgley Jr.'s story is another extremely telling—and rather more dramatic—account of the power of unintended consequences stemming from a single person's actions. His childhood neighbors knew of him as the little Pennsylvanian boy who tinkered in his inventor father's workshop. The world would later come to know him as the mastermind behind General Motors. I think of him as **the King of Unintended Consequences**.

Arguably, Midgley may be one of the most accidentally danger-ous men ever. He has been hailed a "reverse genius" and "the worst inventor in history"—not the sort of legacy any scientist really aims for. Chasing his passion for science and innovation from an early age, Midgley graduated in 1911 from Cornell University with a degree in mechanical engineering. Soon thereafter he joined General Motors. There, he was tasked with addressing one of the company's signifi-cant challenges: engine rattling. He eventually solved this problem by coming up with a solution that became GM's proprietary ethyl lead compound: TEL (tetraethyl lead), which was basically leaded gasoline.

Midgley would hold over 100 patents in his lifetime and received multiple awards for his achievements, but his two most notorious inventions began and ended at GM, with the first reigning as leaded gasoline.

Granted, leading medical experts at the time of TEL's induction warned of potential health problems with this chemical's use, but GM effectively swept these concerns under the rug. It was said that even Midgley would rub the gas along his bare hands to exemplify its safety. Meanwhile, in a plant jointly owned by GM and today's Exxon Mobil, more than 80% of the employees died or suffered from severe lead poi-soning (with symptoms which included bouts of insanity, dubbing this chemical "loony gas"). The world utilized leaded gasoline for decades; it would be many years before society would realize the chemical's massive toxic impact on human health and the environment as a whole; it was finally banned in 1995.

Later in his career, Midgely received a contract by GM's Frigidaire division, with the mission to find a refrigerant alternative to highly flammable ammonia and propane. He helped synthesize dichlorodi-fluoromethane (a.k.a. "Freon"), which is unfortunately composed of carcinogenic chemicals (CFCs) which were later also shown to cause significant damage to the ozone layer. Once again, Midgley's ingenuity, strong work ethic, unfailing optimism, and technical competence in resolving business problems ironically resulted in significantly dangerous unintended consequences. He displayed, as one reporter has later stated, "an absolutely uncanny instinct for doing what we now recognize as the wrong thing, and then building those things into multimillion-dollar industries that would take generations to dismantle."[xlvii]

This isn't to speak ill of Thomas Midgely Jr. On the contrary, he was by most accounts a very intelligent and well-respected scientist who honestly believed in himself as a valuable problem-solver. I cannot know for certain, either, the extent to which he could have foreseen the immense unintended consequences his actions put into motion.

In 1940, in a strange and perhaps karmatic twist of fate, Midgley contracted polio. This disease greatly limited his mobility. Ever the innovator, he built a system of pulleys and levers that allowed him to get out of his bed without assistance. In 1944, at the age of 55—as if in a final testament of tragic irony and backfiring consequences—Midgely was found dead as a result of being strangled by the very cables of the aforementioned system that he himself had created.

In Conclusion: Beware of Blowback

One fun fact about the CIA is that it's got its own term for unintended consequences: **blowback.**

The term was CIA internal coinage to illustrate "the unintended, harmful consequences—to friendly populations and military forces—when a given weapon is used beyond its purpose as intended by the party

xlvii   Stockton, R. (2016, December 21). Thomas Midgley Jr.: Accidentally The Most Dangerous Man Who Ever Lived. Retrieved from http://all-that-is-interesting.com/thomas-midgley-jr.

supplying it."[xlviii] Examples include Osama bin Laden, Salvadorian Civil War banana republic juntas, and ISIS. Merriam-Webster aptly defines *blowback* in more general terms, as "an unforeseen and unwanted effect, result, or set of repercussions."

The first time the term was used regularly by US journalists was in 1975, with specific reference to Chile during Senate Hearings. Reportedly the CIA had spent millions of dollars to plant fake news stories in Chile, and the issue was to investigate how much of this fake news made its way back to the United States media as news. This investigation uncovered the fact that the CIA actually had hundreds of media outlets around the globe; Congressmen wished to investigate how much blowback—in the form of fake stories hitting the US media—actually occurred. Another infamous instance of blowback occurred in the 1970s regarding the covert American intervention between Afghan rebels (including Osama Bin Laden and Sheikh Omar Abdul-Rahman) and the former Soviet Union. It's been suggested that the work done by the CIA to aid the rebels against the Soviets—at a reported cost of over $3 billion—helped empower Afghan groups that were often fundamentalist and anti-American, ultimately resulting in (leading to or being conducive for) the unintended consequences of countless terror attacks and political instability and violence.

There are many lessons to be gleaned from CIA blowback case studies, including how significant it is to consider the long-term impact of your actions. Short-sightedness can be nothing short of devastating. Success lies in balancing a sense of urgency with a sense of discretion to ensure that your "solution" not only answers today's problems but also the concerns of tomorrow. This is critical in the high-stakes world of international security, intelligence, and politics; it applies just as easily in the sphere of business. As demonstrated by the spectrum of this book's case studies, executives who choose to act

---

xlviii   Blowback (intelligence). (2013, April). *Wikipedia.* Retrieved from https://en.wikipedia.org/wiki/Blowback_(intelligence).

with short-sightedness often position themselves and their organizations at a grave disadvantage.

Blowback doesn't occur only when an organization acts unscrupulously—resulting in legal, moral, and ethical repercussions—but even when leaders make perfectly moral and legal decisions that are simply imprudent in the long-term. Consider Blockbuster's decision to pass on a chance to buy Netflix (business blowback stemming from a decision not to act). Or something as simple as cake-maker Entemann's tweeting "who's #notguilty about eating all the tasty treats they want?!"—purely innocent until the company realized that their tweet backfired because the #notguilty hashtag was associated with the 2011 verdict of the Casey Anthony (accused of killing her 2-year-old daughter and later convicted for lying) trial—something they hadn't known and still found themselves apologizing for in a follow-up tweet: "Sorry everyone, we weren't trying to reference the trial in our tweet! We should have checked the trending hashtag first."[xlix]

So, the next time you're faced with a decision—and it may be sooner than you think—take an extra moment (or a few) to deliberate on a few key concerns. Are you seeing the whole picture? Have you considered all aspects and outcomes from as many perspectives as you can gather? Are you focusing on long-term goals or sacrificing them for pettier short-term gain? Do you understand how your target audience may or may not respond? What would your decision be incentivizing? And when unintended consequences do arise, have you cultivated a corporate culture and team that can roll with the punches?

Remember, too, that you have limited capacities and can't fight every battle. Think before you leap, and don't get riled up like Streisand over the small stuff. Pick the battles that would best serve your organization; focus your resources in a manner that is conducive to achieving the cumulative, long-term goals. Sometimes this will mean making an

---

xlix   #Fail: 29 Of The Biggest Corporate Brand Social Media Flubs. (2017, March 17). Retrieved from https://www.cbinsights.com/blog/corporate-social-media-fails/.

informed decision indicative of the fact that sometimes "perfection is the enemy of progress"...and move forward.

To an extent, unintended consequences are inevitable. While it is unreasonable to expect people to be able to predict every possible outcome—especially given the context of the butterfly effect and the complexities of modern society—good leadership means knowing what you can control and when. We are all participants in an advanced economic, political, and social ecosystem that extends far beyond our own; we simply can't have the bandwidth to know everything we need to make the right decision every moment. We will be impacted many times, too, by the unintended consequences resulting from the actions of *other* participants in the market. We won't be able to foresee all external or even internal forces.

Unintended consequences can come weighed with great cost in terms of money, time, energy, and reputation. Guarding against them means being proactive. It's about striving to be the most knowledgeable in your respective corner of the market, about developing risk management strategies, and having well-defined disaster recovery programs. At the heart of it all, it's about your corporate mentality and culture. View failure as a stepping stone to success. Learning and leveraging what you've learned is the hallmark of good leadership.

As leaders, we must learn to share knowledge and to accept it, too; we must leverage the skills of the people on our teams. The stories in this chapter and those found throughout the book also serve to stress the importance of exercising good judgment when the scales of unintended consequences are not tilted in our favor. Remember that unintended consequences may help or hurt you, but it is sound leadership, prudent decision making, good communication, and great teamwork that will dictate your ultimate success or failure.

Acknowledgements

"None of us are greater than the sum of our parts," Eric Hirzel once said. I can attest to that, witnessing and living examples of this quote every day of my life. The older I get, the more I realize that few things of value are ever created by a single individual.

That is truly the case for this book. The process of taking an interesting set of business stories and marrying them to the enduring work of Dr. Merton has been made possible through my collaboration with three amazing people—two of whom I've never met in person, and one with whom I've shared nearly every day with over the past 33 years.

My thanks to **David Zomaya**, who extensively researched and curated the bulk of the stories within this book. David and I began working together before this book was even an inkling of thought. He's been my primary researcher concerning how unintended consequences infest the strategic decisions of senior executives, and he has also sourced me with content for the keynote talks and seminars which I conduct on this subject. He has met every deadline and brought so many fascinating story ideas to me that we had to create a bonus chapter of stories that were simply too good to leave out of this book.

My thanks to **Angela Panayotopulos**, the person I've come to rely on for taking the concepts contained in this book and making them so much more approachable for the reader. Her ability to bring forth the main ideas and best practices in a simple yet compelling manner has made the writing process for me most enjoyable. In Angela, I have a collaborator who knows how to make the right tweaks to bring focus, energy, and humor to this book. Angela knows how to turn a phrase to make a point. I owe a great deal of gratitude to her for the commitment she made to this book from the first day we started collaborating.

My thanks, last but never least, to **Debra Franzi**, the first person I asked to read the finished manuscript of this book. It was her opinion I was most anxious to hear. Every person needs someone in their life who believes in them unconditionally, and I am lucky to have found that person in my wife. Debra has encouraged me to take on new challenges and has supported me when the results did not happen as fast as I had expected. She's helped me get through my own unintended consequences on many occasions. There have been times when it was solely her belief in me that would get me out of bed in the morning and keep my eyes on the prize. Needless to say, I'm overjoyed she likes the manuscript.

About the Author

Experience is the best teacher…but in business, some lessons are best learned vicariously through the experiences of other executives.

Born and bred in a small coal mining and steel mill town in Western Pennsylvania, Richard moved to Orange County, CA, in 1981 after graduating with a B.A. in Communications from the University of Pittsburgh. While in Southern California, he continued his education by attaining his MBA from Pepperdine University in 1992. Today Richard Franzi is the Founder and CEO of **Critical Mass for Business**, established in 2007 and acclaimed as a fast-growth, premium social/peer learning firm for executives who lead firms with annual revenues between $5 million to $50 million. He is a business partner with Renaissance Executive Forums, a leading international advisory board firm founded in 1994.

As a nationally recognized thought leader and a fierce advocate for the power of peer learning specifically for CEOs and business owners, Richard currently chairs **CEO Peer Groups®** throughout Los Angeles and Orange County, CA. His work has been featured in national print and online media, talk shows, publications, and educational forums and outlets. Richard's business talk show, **Critical Mass Radio Show**, showcases over 1,200 interviews available on various podcasting platforms. His direct experience as a member and chair of CEO Peer Groups® has inspired his two prior business books: *Critical Mass: The Power of CEO Guiding Principles* (now in its third release) and *Critical Mass: The 10 Explosive Powers of CEO Peer Groups* (the first book ever written about how executives benefit from the peer group process).

    Killing Cats Leads to Rats is his third book. He is currently conducting extensive research for his fourth publication which will be released in 2018. Richard's personal BHAG—what Jim Collins has coined as the "big hairy audacious goal"—is to positively impact 1 million lives through his work and research. Feel free to connect with him via social media to further explore the power of peer learning.